Fighting With Blade, Bayonet & Staff Weapons

Fighting With Blade, Bayonet & Staff Weapons

Two Guides to the Art of Close Combat

Broad-Sword and Single-Stick

by R. G. Allanson-Winn
and C. Phillipps-Wolley

&

The Art of Fencing

by Monsieur L'Abbat

LEONAUR

Fighting With Blade, Bayonet & Staff Weapons:
Two Guides to the Art of Close Combat

Broad-Sword and Single-Stick
by R. G. Allanson-Winn and C. Phillipps-Wolley

The Art of Fencing
by Monsieur L'Abbat

Published by Leonaur Ltd

ISBN: 978-0-85706-389-2 (hardcover)
ISBN: 978-0-85706-390-8 (softcover)

http://www.leonaur.com

Contents

Broad-Sword and Single-Stick

R. G. Allanson-Winn and
C. Phillipps-Wolley

Preface

The favour with which my little brochure on boxing has been received induces me to put together a few ideas on the subject of attack and defence with weapons other than those with which nature has endowed us.

A glance at the table of contents will suffice to show that the scope of the work has been somewhat extended, and that, though there is of course a vast deal more to be said on the wide subject of self-defence, an attempt has been made to give practical hints as to what may be effected by a proper and prompt use of those common accessories which we may find in our hands at almost any hour in the day.

Not having leisure to take in hand the whole of the work myself, I asked my friend Mr. C. Phillipps-Wolley to make himself responsible for that portion of the treatise which deals with single-stick play. This he kindly consented to do. The illustrations in this portion of the work are from photographs by the London Stereoscopic Company; all the other illustrations are from my own sketches.

The Author

Chapter 1

Introductory

Our neighbours on the other side of the English Channel have been accused of calling us a "nation of shopkeepers." No doubt the definition is not bad; and, so long as the goods supplied bear the hall-mark of British integrity, there is nothing to be ashamed of in the appellation; still, with all due deference, I think we might more appropriately be called a nation of sportsmen.

There is not an English boy breathing at this moment who does not long to be at some sport or game, and who has not his pet idea of the channel into which he will guide his sporting proclivities when he is a man. There are not many grown Englishmen who don't think they know something about a horse, would not like to attend a good assault-at-arms, or who are not pleased when they hear of their sons' prowess with the oar, the bat, or the gloves.

I may be quite mistaken, but it always seems to me that the well-brought-up little foreign boy is too unwholesomely good and gentle to fight the battle of life. Still, such little boys *do* grow up brave and clever men, and they *do*, taken collectively, make splendid soldiers.

Then, as to sports, foreigners seem to put too much pomp and circumstance into their efforts in pursuit of game; the impedimenta and general accoutrements are overdone; but here again I may be wrong.

Of one thing we may be quite sure, and that is that the majority of Englishmen are devoted to sport of *some kind*. One of the prettiest little compliments you can pay a man is to call him "a good old sportsman."

When, in addition to the advantages of a national sport or collection of national sports, such as boxing, sword exercises, wrestling, etc., you recognize the possibility that the games you have been indulging in with your friends in playful contests may at almost any moment be utilized for defeating your enemies and possibly saving your life, you are forced to the conclusion that there are some sports at least which can be turned to practical account.

Unfortunately there are individuals, possibly in the small minority, who regard anything like fighting as brutal or ungentlemanly. In a sense—a very limited sense—they may be right, for, though our environment is such that we can never rest in perfect security, it does seem hard that we should have to be constantly on the alert to protect that which we think is ours by right, and ours alone.

However this may be, let us be men *first*, and aristocrats, gentlemen, or anything else you please, *afterwards*. If we are not men, in the larger and better sense of the word, let there be no talk of gentle blood or lengthy pedigree. The nation is what it is through the pluck and energy of individuals who have put their shoulders to the wheel in bygone days—men who have laid the foundation of a glorious empire by sturdy personal efforts—efforts, unaided by the state, emanating from those higher qualities of the character, relying on itself, and on itself alone, for success or failure.

From the earliest times, and in the most primitive forms of animal life, physical efforts to obtain the mastery have been incessant.

Whether it is in the brute creation or the human race, this struggle for existence has always required the exercise of offensive and defensive powers. The individual has striven to gain his living, and to protect that living when gained; nations have paid armies to increase their territories, and retain those territories when acquired.

The exact form of weapon which first came into use will always be doubtful, but one would think that stones, being hard and handy, as well as plentiful, might have presented irresistible attractions to, say, some antediluvian monster, who wished to intimate to a mammoth or *icthyosaurus*, a few hundred yards distant, his readiness to engage in mortal combat.

Are there not stories, too, of clever little apes in tropical forests who have pelted unwary travellers with nuts, stones, and any missiles which came handy?

Then, coming nearer home, there is the lady at an Irish fair who hangs on the outskirts of a faction-fight, ready to do execution with a stone in her stocking—a terrible *gog-magog* sort of brain-scatterer.

When man was developed, no doubt one of his first ideas was to get hold of a really good serviceable stick—not a little modern masher's crutch—a strong weapon, capable of assisting him in jumping, protecting him from wild beasts, and knocking down his fellow-man.

To obtain such a stick the primitive man probably had to do a good deal of hacking at the bough of a hard oak or tough ash, with no better knife than a bit of sharp flint. Having secured his stick, the next thing was to keep it, and he doubtless had to defend himself against the assaults of envious fellow-creatures possessed of inferior sticks.

Thus we can imagine that the birth of quarter-staff play—not much *play* about it in those days—was a very simple affair; and we recognize in it the origin and foundation of all the sword exercises, and all the games in which single-stick, lance, and bayonet play a prominent part.

As the question of who picked up the first stone and threw it at his fellow-man, or when the first branch of a tree was brought down on the unsuspecting head of another fellow-man, are questions for learned men to decide, and are of no real importance, I shall not allow myself to go on with any vague speculations, but shall turn at once to an old English sport which, though sometimes practised at assaults-at-arms in the present day, takes us back to Friar Tuck, Robin Hood, and

Maid Marian, fair as ivory bone,
Scarlet and Much and Little John.

Chapter 2

The Quarter-Staff

According to *Chambers's Encyclopaedia*, the quarter-staff was "formerly a favourite weapon with the English for hand-to-hand encounters." It was "a stout pole of heavy wood, about six and a half feet long, shod with iron at both ends. It was grasped in the middle by one hand, and the attack was made by giving it a rapid circular motion, which brought the loaded ends on the adversary at unexpected points."

"Circular motion" and "shod with iron" give a nasty ring to this description, and one pictures to one's self half a barge-pole, twirled—"more Hibernico"—with giant fingers, bearing down on one.

Whether the fingers of our ancestors were ever strong enough to effect this single-handed twirling or not must remain a matter of doubt, but we may rest assured that in the quarter-staff we have, probably, the earliest form of offensive weapon next to the handy stone. If Darwin is correct, we can easily imagine one of our gorilla ancestors picking up a big branch of a tree with which to hit some near member of his family. This, to my mind, would be playing elementary quarter-staff, and the game would have advanced a step if the assaulted one—possibly the lady gorilla—had seized another branch and retaliated therewith.

The modern quarter-staff is supposed to be rather longer than the six and a half feet prescribed by the above-quoted authority, and I imagine it originally derived its name from being grasped with one hand at a quarter of its length from the middle, and with the other hand at the middle.

Thus, in the diagram (Fig. 1), if A E represents a quarter-staff eight feet long, divided into four equal two-foot lengths at the points B, C, and D, the idea would be to grasp it with the right hand at D and with the left hand at C; or, if the player happened to be left-handed, to grasp it with the left hand at B and with the right hand at C.

FIG. 1

This method of holding the quarter-staff may be well enough in certain cases, but it seems to me that, for rapid attack and defence, the hands should be about three feet apart: at D and M, half way between B and C; or at B and N, half way between C and D.

Of course a great deal depends upon the height and strength of the player, but, with the hands at a distance of three feet or so apart, it stands to reason you have a greater command over the ends of the staff than you have if they are only two feet apart, and that you can consequently come quicker into "hanging guard" positions, and more easily defend yourself from short upper strokes and from "points" than you can when you have less command over your weapon.

FIG. 2.—ON GUARD

Before proceeding to the more technical portions of quarter-staff play, let me say that it is better to bar "points" in a friendly bout, for the weight of a stick, if only a bamboo cane, of eight feet long, is so great, that it is an easy matter to break a collar-bone or rib with a rapid thrust. In any case, remember to be well padded and to have a good iron-wire broad-sword mask on before engaging in a bout.

In dealing with the cuts and thrusts which may be made with the quarter-staff, we cannot do better than consider the ordinary broad-sword target.

In the accompanying diagram are marked the ordinary broad-sword cuts 1 to 4, 2 to 3, 3 to 2, 4 to 1, 5 to 6, 6 to 5, and 7 to 0, the centre of the target.

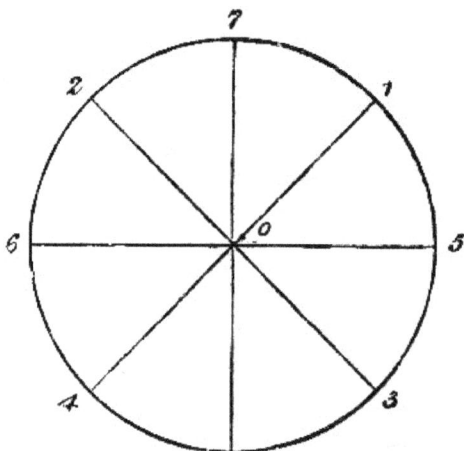

FIG. 3

Now, we observe that the guards for these cuts must be such as to ward off the blows in the easiest manner and with as rapid return as possible to the attacking position.

With the quarter-staff in the hands of a right-handed man, the first cut would be from 2 to 3, and the guard for this would be with the staff held in the direction of c to d. Similarly, for cut two, from 1 to 4, the guard would be from a to b.

It must be borne in mind that this second cut, from 1 to 4, is generally delivered with what I shall call the butt of the staff, *i.e.* with that end which is nearest the right hand, in the case of a right-handed man; and that cut one, from 2 to 3, would be delivered with the butt in the case of a left-handed man.

The two guards above illustrated will *almost* cover any attack, but *not quite*.

FIG. 4.—FIRST HIT

On examining Fig. 8 it will be seen that the guard for the first cut, viz. that from 2 to 3 on the target, is indicated by the position of the staff *cd* or *c'd'*. The guard *cd* meets the three cuts 6 to 5, 2 to 3, and 7 to 0, but is not sufficient to protect you against cut 4 to 1.

Similarly the guard *c'd'* answers the purpose as far as cuts 4 to 1, 6 to 5, and 2 to 3 are concerned, but fails to ward off cut 7 to 0; and the same remarks apply to the other side of the target, where *ab* and *a'b'* represent the staff.

Of course the two guards in Fig. 5 *may* be so used as to meet

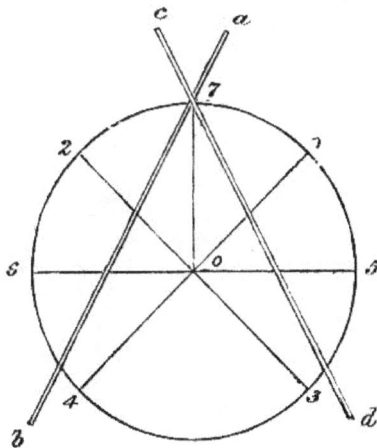

FIG. 5

all requirements, but it is, to my thinking, far preferable to thoroughly master the four as represented in Fig. 9. So doing will give increased command over the staff, and will not in any way detract from speed or general efficiency.

It will be observed that in the sketches of guard 1 and guard 2, Figs. 6 and 7, the staff is, in each case, too perpendicular for cut 7 to 0; they represent the positions of the combatants when using guards $a'b'$ and $c'd'$ in Fig. 8.

FIG. 6.—FIRST GUARD   FIG. 7.—SECOND GUARD

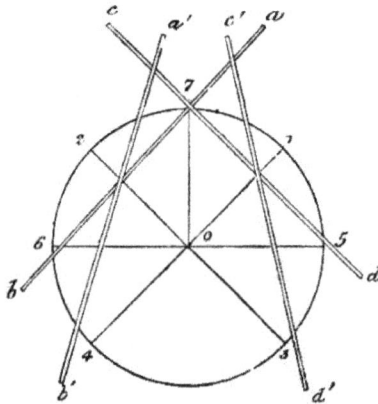

FIG. 8

I would therefore advise attention to the following diagram, which includes the guards, four in number, which are really sufficient for all hits which can be made with the quarter-staff.

18

The lines intersecting the circumference of the circle show the inclinations of the staff for guarding all the cuts which can be made.

We now turn to the question of position. In quarter-staff play it is usual for a right-handed man to stand with his left foot in advance of the right, as in boxing or bayonet exercise, and with his toe pointing straight in the direction of his adversary, as in Fig. 2. It is, however, often very advisable to advance the right foot suddenly to the front when bringing the butt of the staff to play on the left side of the enemy's head or body. As regards "points" it is well to lunge out, as one does when making a left-handed lead-off in boxing, so as to gain somewhat in the reach.

Points, which, as before hinted, should be used with care in friendly bouts, are generally made with the point of the staff, but may also be effected with the butt; and this is the case when the combatants have come to rather close quarters.

At quarter-staff play the men should be started by the Master of Ceremonies at a distance of ten or twelve feet apart, and when they get to close quarters, or at rough play, they should be immediately separated, as this is a game at which feeling is apt to run somewhat high—occasionally.

Always remember, when guarding points, to do so with that portion of the staff which lies between your hands. This portion really corresponds with the "forte" of a sword or stick. If you have learned fencing with the foils it will be of the greatest possible advantage to you, for you will then understand how slight an effort brought to bear on the foible of your opponent's staff—in this case it will be somewhere within two feet of the end—will suffice to turn aside the most vigorous thrust.

It may not be out of place to add that any man who has gone through any sort of apprenticeship in fencing—either with foils or single-sticks—will not fail, when a quarter-staff is put into his hands, to know what to do with his weapon. He may, at first, feel awkward, and the length of the staff may hamper him and its weight fatigue him, but he will, with his knowledge of general principles, very soon get into the work and enjoy it.

Though the staves used are often made of light bamboo cane, one may get very severe hits and prods, so it is as well, before engaging in an encounter, to have (a) a good mask, such as broad-

19

FIG. 9.—SECOND HIT

FIG. 10.—POINT

swordsmen wear; (*b*) a thick jacket of stout leather, with a high collar; (*c*) boxing-gloves on both hands; (*d*) a good pad for the middle of the body, from waist to knee; and (*e*) cricket pads for both legs, which are apt to come in for nasty jars on or about the knee. Never *on any account try to dispense with the pads*—they may save you from permanent injury; and do they not add to your good health by promoting a beneficial opening of the sweat-glands?

In quarter-staff, as in stick-play, broad-sword exercise, fencing, etc., it is better to sink down with the knees bent, for in this position you present a smaller area for your opponent to strike at than you do when quite erect.

In leading off it is better to slide the hand which is at M or N (see Fig. 11) down to the hand which is at D or B; you then gain several feet of reach added to your lunge out; only be careful to recover quickly, and get the hand you have thus moved back to its former position.

Advancing and retreating are effected much in the same way as in bayonet exercise; viz. for the advance, move the left foot swiftly forward in the direction of your opponent for a distance of, say, eighteen inches or two feet, following this up with the right foot *for the same distance*, so that the same relative positions are maintained; for the retreat, move the right foot back the required distance and follow up with the left foot.

In speaking of the retreat, it must be mentioned that, from the great length of the staff, you cannot, very often, get out of the way by the ordinary retreat, as above described, but may have to make an undignified jump back for five or six feet, to avoid a quick return or, possibly, an unexpected lead-off. In a stiff bout this jumping, with all the heavy impedimenta indispensable to the game, takes it out of one considerably, and, on this account, it is a first-rate exercise for any man who may wish to get into good training.

FIG. 11.—FIRST HIT, WITH SLIDE

The most common mistake learners of the quarter-staff make is that they try very long sweeping hits, which are easily guarded, instead of shorter and sharper taps, which run up points and are much more scientific. Your sweeping hit may be likened to the "hook-hit" at boxing, for it lays open your weak points and leaves you for an instant in a position from which there is a difficulty in recovery.

In all these games be well "pulled together." Watch a good fencer, either with the foils or with the sticks; see how seldom his point wanders far from the lines of attack, and how quick he is with the returns! You cannot guard and return with any sort of effect if you go in for ugly sweeping hits or hard heavy guards.

The heavy hit may come off occasionally, the clumsy guard may turn the point, but why misdirect energy? It is surely unnecessary to put forth great muscular effort when you know that the strength of a small child, *if properly applied*, is ample to put aside the most powerful thrust or the heaviest cut.

If quite unacquainted with fencing, broad-sword, stick-play, or bayonet-exercise, never be tempted into a bout with the quarter-staff. No one should ever go in for this game without previous knowledge.

My own idea is that learning fencing with the foils should precede all the above-named exercises, for in this way a delicacy of touch and nicety in the matter of guarding are acquired, which may lay a really good foundation.

Nearly all first-rate stick-players have served their apprenticeship with the foils, and, where this education has been omitted, one may generally detect the ugly carving-knife-and-fork style, so unpleasant to watch. Whereas with a good fencer—"foiler" perhaps I should say—everything is done with neatness, whether he has in his hand a single-stick, a cutlass, or the leg of an old chair.

So that it comes to this: We seek the aid of the newest and most delicate weapon of attack and defence—the small-sword—to teach us how to properly make use of the most ancient and clumsy of all weapons—the time-honoured quarter-staff!

CHAPTER 3

The Broad-Sword

But swords I smile at, weapons laugh to scorn,
Brandish'd by man that's of a woman born.
Macbeth, Act V., Scene vii.

GENERAL

In the early stages of the world's history our very remote ancestors were unacquainted with the art of forging instruments and weapons from metals; they were not even aware of the existence of those metals, and had to content themselves with sharpened flints and other hard stones for cutting purposes. Many of these weapons were fashioned with considerable skill, and give evidence that even in the dark days of the Stone Age men had a good idea of *form* and the adaptation of the roughest materials to suit the particular purpose they had in view.

To take an example from the most common forms—the spear and javelin-heads which are found along with the bones and other remains of the cave bear. These are admirably designed for entering the body of any animal; for, though varying greatly in size, weight, and shape, the double edge and sharp point render them capable of inflicting severe wounds, and of entering into the flesh almost as easily as the point of a modern sword. As good specimens of these early spear-heads fetched high prices, *finding* them was at one time quite a profession, like finding bullets, etc., on the field of Waterloo. Forgeries became common, and in many cases the imitations were so perfect that the most experienced antiquary was often puzzled to pick out the genuine article when placed next to the spurious.

For the benefit of those who take an interest in this branch of research, it may be mentioned that the museum at Salisbury is full of excellent specimens both of true spear-heads and the copies "made to meet the demand," and I may fairly say that the ordinary observer would be utterly incapable of distinguishing the slightest difference between the two.

The genus "cutting instrument," then, has for its archetype the sharp flint, which was fashioned by dint of hard labour in the very early days of man's existence on the face of the earth.

When metals were discovered and their malleability had been tested by the application of fire, not only spear and javelin-heads were formed from the new material, but short swords, consisting entirely of metal, were first constructed; and this departure marked a new era in the civilization of the world, termed by geologists and antiquarians the Bronze Age.

In a very short treatise on a cut-and-thrust weapon like the broad-sword, it would be out of place to enter into any specula-tions as to the probable dates at which the stone, the bronze, and the iron ages commenced their respective epochs. It seems suf-ficient to give the *order* and to mention a few of the early weap-ons with which we are acquainted, either through actually finding them, or by seeing representations of them on early works of art, such as *alto-relievos* or *frescoes*.

One of the earliest forms of sword was the leaf-shaped blade of the early Greeks. It properly belongs to the Bronze Age, as it is found amongst the human remains of that period. It was a short, heavy-bladed weapon, with sharp point and double edge, used, it appears from ancient monuments, for cutting purposes.

FIG. 12.—EARLY GREEK SWORD

No doubt the weight of the blade, increased by the heavy deep ridge running almost from point to hilt, made it very serviceable for cutting, but it seems more than probable that the point was also used, and that the idea of the edge was handed down to us because the ancient sculptor or delineator, in his battle-piece representations, placed the swordsman in the most spirited positions he could think of. A figure in the act of delivering a slashing cut, say cut 1 or cut 2, looks much more aggressive and eager for the fray than a similar figure about to give the point.

I only advance this as a suggestion, for it seems hard to believe that people who must have been well acquainted with the use of the point at the end of a pole or staff—as in the case of the spear, which was the very earliest form of thrusting weapon—should abandon it when they came to the sword.

Be this as it may, there is no doubt that the short Roman sword, which was practically a large heavy dagger, sharp-pointed, double-edged, and straight-bladed, was extensively used for thrusting. For cutting purposes, however, it could not, from the absence of curve in the edge of the blade, have been equal to the early Greek weapon.

FIG. 13.—SHORT ROMAN SWORD

When iron began to play a prominent part in the construction of articles requiring hardness, strength, and durability, a great stride was made in the production of war-like weapons, and it was then very soon discovered that ordinary forged iron was too soft and easily bent, and it was not until the art of tempering began to be roughly understood that iron, or more correctly speaking steel, swords were brought to a degree of perfection sufficient to entitle them to a higher place than their bronze predecessors.

It is believed that the Egyptians had some method of tempering their bronze chisels, which is now numbered amongst the lost arts; otherwise, how could they have carved the head of the Sphinx and innumerable other works out of the intensely hard stone of which so many of their monuments are cut?

The modern sword blade is constructed of steel, tempered so as to suit the particular kind of work for which it is intended. The *Encyclopaedia Britannica* says:

Mechanical invention has not been able to supersede or equal handwork in the production of good sword blades. The swordsmiths' craft is still, no less than it was in the Middle Ages, essentially a handicraft, and it requires a high order of skill. His rough material is a bar of cast and hammered steel, tapering from the centre to the ends; when this is cut in two each half is made into a sword. The 'tang,' which fits into the handle, is not part of the blade, but a piece of wrought iron welded on to its base. From this first stage to the finishing of the point it is all hammer and anvil work. Special tools are used to form grooves in the blade, according to the regulation or other pattern desired, but the shape and weight of the blade are fixed wholly by the skilled hand and eye of the smith. Measuring tools are at hand, but are little used. Great care is necessary to avoid over-heating the metal, which would produce a brittle crystalline grain, and to keep the surface free from oxide, which would be injurious if hammered in. In tempering the blade the workman judges of the proper heat by the colour. Water is preferred to oil by the best makers, notwithstanding that tempering in oil is much easier. With oil there is not the same risk of the blade coming out distorted and having to be forged straight again (a risk, however, which the expert swordsmith can generally avoid); but the steel is only surface-hardened, and the blade therefore remains liable to bend. Machinery comes into play only for grinding and polishing, and to some extent in the manufacture of hilts and appurtenances. The finished blade is proved by being caused to strike a violent blow on a solid block, with the two sides flat, with the edge, and lastly with the back; after this the blade is bent flatwise in both directions by hand, and finally the point is driven through a steel plate about an eighth of an inch thick. In spite of all the care that can be used, both in choice of materials and in workmanship, about forty *per cent.* of the blades thus tried fail to stand the proof and are rejected. The process we have briefly described is that of making a really good sword; of course plenty of cheaper and commoner weapons are in the market, but they are hardly fit to trust a man's life to. It is an interesting fact that the peculiar skill of the swordsmith is in England so far hereditary that it can be traced back in the same families for several generations.

The best Eastern blades are justly celebrated, but they are not better than the best European ones; in fact, European swords are often met with in Asiatic hands, remounted in Eastern fashion. The 'damascening' or 'watering' of choice Persian and Indian is not a secret of workmanship, but is due to the peculiar manner of making the Indian steel itself, in which a crystallizing process is set up; when metal of this texture is forged out, the result is a more or less regular wavy pattern running through it. No difference is made by this in the practical qualities of the blade.

The above-quoted description, though short and superficial, is sufficient to indicate some of the chief difficulties of the sword-smith's art, and it sets one thinking, too, as to the various uses to which cutting instruments are put, and gradations of hardness, from the high temper of razors and certain chisels to the low temper of hunters' and sailors' knives, which should always be of rather soft steel, for they are sharpened more easily, and the saw-like edge is better suited for cutting flesh, ropes, etc., than a very fine edge would be.

A comparatively soft steel does well enough for the heavy cut-lass used for cutting lead or dividing a sheep, and the edge, though sharp and keen, need not, and, indeed, cannot, approach the razor-edge necessary for cutting a silk pocket-handkerchief or a feather.

Every edge, when closely examined by a microscope, presents a more or less saw-like and jagged appearance. It is merely a ques-tion of *degree*, and, in a sword to be used for ordinary cutting and thrusting, you want to secure hardness sufficient to produce a good edge and an instant return to its former shape after any reasonable bending, and you want to avoid anything like brittle-ness or liability to snap. If the disposition of the molecules is such as to give too great hardness, the blade, though capable of taking a fine edge, will probably snap, or the edge will crack and shiver on meeting any hard obstacle. For example, if you put razor steel into a cutlass, and then try to cut lead, the blade will either snap off or the edge will break away in large pieces. If, on the other hand, you make the blade of too soft steel, the edge will be readily dented or turned on one side.

Though there are wonderful reports of the excellence of Eastern blades manufactured at Damascus, it is probable that European work was quite as good, and that the tempering of steel was quite as well understood at Toledo, in Spain, where, in the sixteenth and seventeenth centuries, splendid rapiers were produced. It seems highly probable that the rapier was an extension or refinement of the earlier heavy cut-and-thrust sword, because, though the superior value of the point was beginning then to assert itself, there was an evident attempt to preserve in the rapier the strength and cutting properties of the long straight sword of a previous time.

The Italian and Spanish rapiers were sometimes of great length, three feet or three feet six inches and more in the blade, and they were often beautifully finished, the work of the hilts being frequently both elaborate and costly. The blade itself, which was double-edged and inclined to be flat, tapered gradually from hilt to point, and was strengthened by a ridge running almost its entire length.

The French duelling-sword of modern days is sometimes spoken of as a "rapier;" but this is incorrect, as the popular Gallic dispute-settler is three-sided, and is, as it has no edge, exclusively used for pointing.

For *details* of historical research, and other particulars, the reader is referred to Mr. Egerton Castle's work on the sword.

THE MODERN CUT-AND-THRUST SWORD

The word "Broad-sword" may be taken to include all kinds of cut-and-thrust swords. It is the generic term for ship's cutlass, infantry sword, and heavy cavalry sabre, which are all cutting weapons, and, though varying in length and curvature of blade, can be used for pointing.

The method of holding the broad-sword depends entirely upon the weight and length of the blade. If you have a light cutlass weighing, say, about one and a half pound, and measuring about thirty-four inches in the blade, you may hold it in the same way as in single-stick play, *viz.* with the thumb on the back of the hilt, as in the sketch, and you will probably find that in this way the guards are made with greater facility. At the same time, when guarding, say, with the hanging guard (see Fig. 15), the thumb is liable to a severe

FIG. 14.—GRIP FOR THE LIGHT CUTLASS

FIG. 15—LOW HANGING GUARD

sprain; and this is more particularly the case when the opposing blade meets the foible, or half nearest the point of your blade, at right angles, or nearly so.

To be more explicit. If A B C, in Fig. 16, represent your blade lying flat on the paper, *d o* the intersection of a plane at right angles to the plane of the paper and also at right angles to the tangent to the curve at the point *o*, where we will suppose the edges of the

29

blades to meet, it will be seen at a glance that the leverage from *o* to C is considerable, and that a great strain is thrown upon the thumb which is endeavouring to keep the guard in position.

In this case the cut has been received on the "foible," or half of the blade nearest the point. All guards should, if possible, be made with the "forte," or half nearest the hilt.

It is important to bear in mind that the cut should be received with the guard as much as possible on the slant; *i.e.* you should endeavour to make the opponent's blade glance off yours at an angle such as *d′ o*. The difficulty of bringing about this "glance off" is certainly increased by having the thumb on the hilt, because your hanging guard—which is perhaps the most important and constantly recurring of all the guards—is apt to be higher, *so far as the point is concerned*, and there is the chance of letting in cuts 3 or 5 at the left side, which is exposed by an elevated point.

If, in the hanging guard, the arm is well extended, with the hand slightly above the level of the shoulder, the point dropped well to the left, and the edge turned outwards to the left, as in the illustration (Fig. 15), a very good general guard will be formed. Remember, too, that in all cuts, points, or guards, the second knuckles of the fingers should be in a line with the edge. The only exception to this rule is, perhaps, to be found in the third point, where a shifting of the hand, so as to enable the edge to be more completely directed upwards, is sometimes recommended.

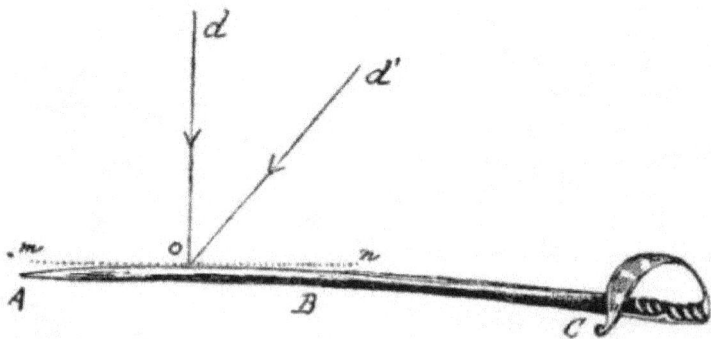

FIG. 16—THE BROAD-SWORD

The hanging guard, or modifications thereof, is capable of warding off all cuts made at the left side of the head and body, and is also effective against cut 7. Then, by bringing the hand slightly to the right, with the elbow held well in to the right side, it is extremely easy to come into the position for guarding cut 2.

We may, I think, assume that, on the whole, the thumb held at the back of the hilt gives, in the case of a very light sword, an advantage in speed, especially with short quick cuts and points.

Turning to the heavy sabre used by the cavalry of this and other countries, we observe that to keep the thumb on the back of the hilt would lead to constant sprains. No man is strong enough to wield with effect a blade weighing about two and a half pounds and measuring little short of three feet—thirty-five inches is the regulation length of the British cavalry sabre—unless he holds it as indicated in Fig. 17.

FIG. 17.—GRIP FOR THE HEAVY SABRE

Most cuts made with the heavy sword are more sweeping in their nature, more "swinging," so to speak, than the short quick cuts which can be effected with the lighter and more handy weapon; indeed, it is only to be expected that the weight of the blade and length of the sweep should give great force to the sabre; but it must not be forgotten that what is thus gained in power is lost in speed, and that in nine cases out of ten a well-directed "point" would be immeasurably superior both in speed and effect than the most sweeping cut.

Such very different weapons are required to be thoroughly effective in different circumstances. A light, thin-bladed sword, though admirable for a man on foot, would not be of nearly so much use to a cavalry man, whose slashing cut through shield or helmet renders *weight* an absolute necessity. The light blade might be brought to bear with all the speed and force of the strongest man, but would be of no avail in those cases where hard, dense, and heavy substances have to be cut through.

A fly may dash against a pane of plate-glass with the utmost speed and yet fail to break the glass; but a cricket-ball thrown with a tenth part of the velocity will smash the window to pieces. This is only an analogous case, which indicates very fully the existence of the two factors in the *vis-viva* necessary to produce a certain result.

If you get your blade too light it will not be serviceable for heavy-cutting work, whatever the speed of the cut; and if you get the blade too heavy, it will be impossible to use it effectively on account of its weight.

Everything depends upon what a sword is expected to do; and in selecting a blade this cannot be too carefully borne in mind.

The Easterns have not, and indeed never had, any idea of using the point; but they are far and away our superiors at edge work, and their curved scimitars are admirably adapted for effective cutting, because the edge, meeting the object aimed at on the slant, has great cutting or slicing power.

This brings us to the most important matter in connection with cutting weapons—the "draw."

If you take a razor in one hand and *hit* the palm of the other hand a smart *blow* with the edge, no harm will be done; but if you vary this hit, by making it lighter and putting the slightest possible *draw* into it, a cut will be the result, and blood will flow freely. That is to say, anything like *drawing* the edge along the skin will produce a cut.

Turn to the case of the scimitar. It will be seen that the curved form of the blade *from hilt to point* renders it impossible for a sweeping cut, given with the arm extended its full length and with the shoulder as centre of the circle, which the hand traces out in making the cut, to be other than a "draw," because the edge *must* meet the object to be severed on the slant.

Excellent examples of this kind of cutting are to be found in the circular saw and the chaff-cutting machine.

FIG. 18.—THE SCIMITAR

But this is not the case with a nearly straight-bladed broad-sword, which requires what may be termed an artificial draw, either backward or forward, in order that the cut may have its full effect. Of course the draw back is by far the most common form of the "draw;" and on reference to the accompanying sketch (Fig. 19) it will be seen that the edge, if the hand retains its position *throughout the entire sweep*, on the circumference of the circle B D, will meet the object to be cut simply as a *hit*, and not as a *cut*. This is just what we want to avoid.

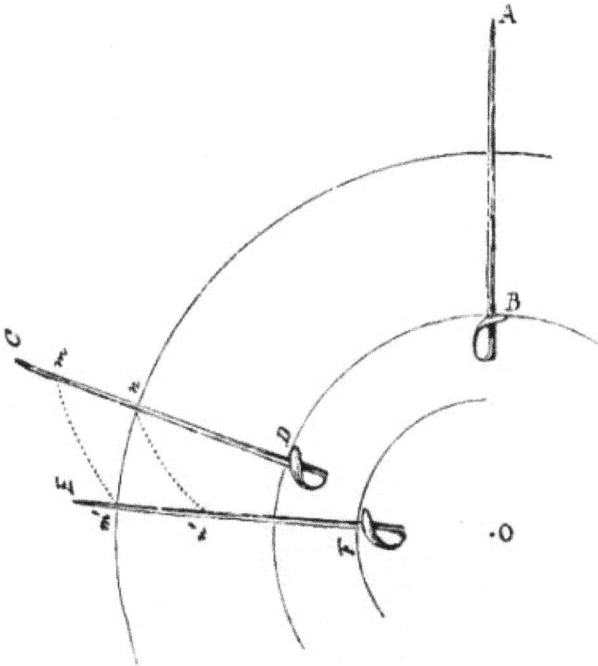

FIG. 19

Suppose the cut is being made parallel to the plane of the paper, and that the hilt of the sword is, in the first part of the sweep, moving on the circumference of the circle from B to D. Suppose,

33

too, that the edge first meets the obstacle to be cut at the point *n*. Then slightly before *n* is reached the "draw" should commence, the hand coming into position at F, and the point *n* being necessarily drawn down to *n'* by the time the object has been severed. That is to say, the portion of the blade between *m* and *n* will have been made effective in the drawing cut, the point *n* having travelled in the direction of the dotted lines till it arrives at *n'*.

The point *n* is taken at random: it might be nearer the hilt or nearer the point, according to the distance of the object aimed at. It may also be observed that the "draw" *might* continue during the entire sweep from B to F, but a very slight consideration will show clearly the advantage of keeping the arm fully extended until the edge is quite close to the object, as, by this means, the reach is increased and the *power of the cut gains considerably*. The dynamical proof of this latter advantage would take up too much space, and I regret that it is rather outside the scope of this little work.

No matter how extended the arm may be when commencing the cut—and the more extended the better in the case of a long heavy sword—the "draw" should always come in towards the end of the sweep, the first part of which is merely intended to give the required impetus to the effective portion of the cut.

How is it that an apple or potato can be divided by a straight cut when placed in the folds of a silk pocket-handkerchief, which remains uninjured? Simply because there is a complete absence of "draw," and the apple or potato is broken or split in two, much as the flesh is indented by the edge of the razor whilst the skin escapes without the slightest mark.

In cavalry charges, etc., our soldiers too often forget that they have in their hands *pointing* and *cutting* weapons, and make slashing *hits*, which lead to a large percentage of broken blades. I should myself always place the point before the edge, as it is quicker and far more deadly; but as there are numerous instances where cutting is necessary, it is as well to remember that a mere *hit* with the true edge of a straight-bladed sword is little better than a blow from a heavy stick having an oval section. This brings us to another very important part of the subject, *viz.* the consideration of the best form of weapon for ordinary practice.

To many it may seem that in these few pages on swordsmanship the cart has been placed before the horse, and that a discussion on cuts and guards should have preceded the somewhat intricate questions we have been considering. I have, however, thought it advisable to leave what may be termed the "drudgery" to the end of the chapter, in the hope of thereby creating a more lively interest in the subject. It must, nevertheless, be remembered that, to attain to any sort of proficiency with the sword, a long apprenticeship must be served.

Though stick-play is invaluable as an aid to work with the sword, it may be remarked that there are two reasons, and those important ones, why the single-stick should not be first placed in the hands of the beginner, and why it should never altogether usurp the place of the more lethal weapon. The reasons are—

(*a.*) The stick is very light, and short smart hits can be made, which are impossible with a sword.

(*b.*) The hit with the stick is really a hit, and there need be no draw, which, as already explained, is so important in sword-play.

To these may be added a third reason. With the stick there is always the temptation not to cut with the true edge, and it is very hard to detect faults in this direction—faults which are hard to cure, and which may quite spoil good swordsmanship.

Remembering, then, that every cut and guard must be made with the true edge, and with the second or middle knuckles of the fingers in the direction of the edge, a navy cutlass may be placed in the beginner's hand, and he may be gradually taught all the cuts and guards by means of the target, a sketch of which is here given.

In the manual on sword-exercises at present in use in the army, it is stated that there are "four cuts and four guards, so arranged for the sake of clearness, though practically there are only two cuts— from right to left and from left to right, high and low—and two guards, one a variation of the 'hanging' or 'engaging guard,' formed high or low, right or left, according to the part attacked, and the other the 'second guard,' where the point of the sword is necessarily directed upwards, to guard the right cheek and shoulder."

This is very brief, and, to my mind, the effort to be concise has tended to somewhat confuse. It may, however, be well enough for the army, where there are plenty of instructors ready to explain the meanings of terms, etc. For ordinary beginners it is certainly bet-

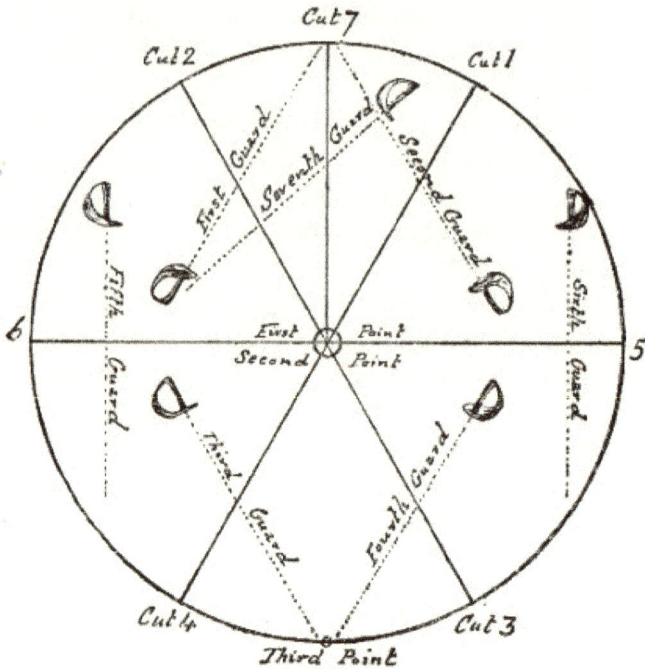

FIG. 20.—THE TARGET

ter to take the old target and thoroughly master the seven cuts and three points, with the corresponding guards and parries, as by so doing the learner will more readily acquire a thorough appreciation of true edge-cutting. The general statement that there are two cuts—*viz.* variations from right to left, and variations from left to right—is correct enough, and a swordsman understands it; but it is bad for beginners to start with loose notions on the subject. Better far learn all the cuts, and learn them *well*, in the first instance. By this means a man and his sword become one, as it were, and the point and edge of the weapon are in time brought so completely under control that they can be directed as easily as the pencil and brush are directed by the hand of a skilful draughtsman.

As the reader will have surmised, the lines drawn through the centre of the circle indicate the directions of the cuts; but a little further explanation is necessary, for it must not be supposed that a mere following of these lines with the point of the sword is all that is required. The flat of the blade (or, more accurately, a plane passing through the edge and a line drawn down the centre of the back of the blade from hilt to point) should, throughout the entire cut, coincide with the plane intersecting the plane of the target at right angles in the particular line in which the cut is being made.

Careful attention to this will ensure cutting with the true edge, and, in the first instance, all the cuts should be made slowly and deliberately, so that errors may be instantly corrected. This may be somewhat tedious to the impetuous learner, but it really saves time in the end.

The target should be hung up on a wall with the centre about the height of a man's shoulder from the ground. Directly below the centre a straight line should be drawn on the ground from the wall, and at right angles to it.

The beginner should be stationed on this line in the position of "Attention," at about nine or ten feet from the wall, so that when he comes into the first position of the exercise his right foot may be on the line, and may point directly towards the wall.

Instructions as to drawing swords, etc., will be given later on with the Extension Motions and rules for loose play. At this stage it may possibly be less confusing to merely give the following positions, leaving to the concluding portions of the chapter a few amplifications which may materially assist the swordsman when he has begun to take a genuine interest in the subject.

Attention.—Having taken the cutlass in the right hand, stand facing the target, body and head erect, and the heels close together and meeting at an angle of sixty degrees on the line drawn from the wall.

With the sword hand in front of, and on a level with, the elbow, which should be close to the body, and with the blade pointing perpendicularly upwards with the edge to the front, you will be in the position of "Carry swords." Now relax the grasp of the last three fingers, and, without altering the position of the hand, let the back of the blade fall on the shoulder half-way between the neck and the point of the shoulder. This forms the position of "Slope swords," with which the exercise begins.

First Position.—Bring the right heel before the left; feet at right angles, right foot pointing towards target; shoulders square to left, and weight of body chiefly resting on left leg.

Second Position.—Bend both knees, keeping them well apart, without raising the heels or altering the erect position of the body. Step out with the right foot along the line for about eighteen or twenty inches straight in direction of the target, still retaining most of the weight of the body on the left leg.

Third Position.—Step out still further along the line—about a yard or so (according to the height of the individual)—keeping the shin-bone as nearly as possible perpendicular to the instep. The left leg should be straight and the left heel should not leave the ground. The heels should be both on the line, and the shoulders should be square to the left; *i.e.* the right shoulder should be well extended and the left held back. The weight is now, of course, principally on the right leg.

At the word "Attention," then, the pupil should come into the position of "Slope swords," already described.

Prepare for Sword Exercise.—Turning on the heels, come into the "first position," with the left forearm well behind the back and the hand closed.

Right, Prove Distance.—Bring the upper part of the hilt of the sword on a level with the mouth, blade pointing perpendicularly upwards, edge to the left, and the elbow close to the side. This forms the position "Recover swords." Now extend the arm to the right, and lower the blade in a horizontal position straight out from the right shoulder, edge to the rear, shoulders square to the front, and the head and eyes turned to the right in the direction in which the sword is pointing.

Return to the position "Slope swords."

Front, Prove Distance.—"Recover swords" as before, and, extending the arm with the point of the sword directed towards the centre of the target, step out into the third position, taking care that the edge is towards the right.

Return to the position "Slope swords."

In proving distance Right and Front, the forefinger and thumb may be stretched along the handle of the hilt, the thumb being on the back and the pommel of the hilt in the palm of the hand.

Assault.—Come into First Position; raise the right arm to the front with the wrist opposite No. 1 and the elbow rather bent, and inclining towards the centre of the target, the back of the blade, near the point, resting on the shoulder, with the edge inclined to the right.

Cut One.—With an extension of the arm direct the cut diagonally from No. 1 to No. 4 (*remembering in this, and all the following cuts, to use the true edge*), and as the point clears the circle, turn the knuckles upwards, continuing the sweep of the sword until the point comes to the rear of the left shoulder, with edge to the left and the wrist opposite No. 2.

Cut Two.—Now cut diagonally from left to right from No. 2 to No. 3. Continue the motion till the arm is extended to the right, on a level with the shoulder, edge to the rear.

Cut Three.—Now turn the wrist so that the knuckles and edge face to the front, and cut diagonally upwards from No. 3 to No. 2, and continue the sweep until the wrist rests in the hollow of the left shoulder, with the point of the sword pointing upwards and the edge to the rear; turn the wrist so that the edge faces to the front, and drop the point until the blade is in the position for the next cut.

Cut Four.—Cut diagonally upwards from No. 4 to No. 1 until the blade is nearly perpendicular, edge and knuckles to the rear. Bring the arm, still fully extended, to the position of "Right, prove distance," and turn the wrist so that the knuckles and edge face to the front, the blade being horizontal and on a level with the shoulders.

Cut Five.—Cut horizontally from No. 5 to No. 6. The edge will now be to the left and the point to the rear, over the left shoulder.

Cut Six.—Turn the wrist so that knuckles and edge face to the front, and cut horizontally from No. 6 to No. 5. Continuing the sweep until the hand is nearly over the head and in the direction of No. 7, the sword being on the same line over the head, point lowered to the rear, and the edge directed vertically upwards.

Cut Seven.—Cut vertically downwards from No. 7 to the centre of the target, and remain with the arm extended.

First Point.—Turn the wrist, with the edge of the sword upwards, to the right. Bring the hand upwards on a level with the eyes, elbow bent and raised, the point of the sword directed towards the centre of the target, and the left shoulder advanced. Now, by an extension of the arm, deliver the point smartly to the front, with the edge of the sword still inclined upwards to the right and the point accurately directed to the centre. The right shoulder should now be well advanced and the left drawn back—this motion of the shoulders being applicable to all the points.

Second Point.—Turn the edge upwards to the left, draw the elbow close to the body and let the wrist be as high as, and in front of, the left breast. Now deliver the point, as before directed, accurately towards the centre of the target, the wrist inclining towards No. 2.

Third Point.—Draw in the arm till the inside of the wrist touches the right hip, the edge being raised upwards to the right, the left shoulder slightly advanced and the hips well thrown back. Now deliver the point accurately towards the lowest point on the target, the edge being carefully directed upwards to the right throughout the motion.

Guards.—Having gone through the cuts and points, the pupil should now give his attention to the guards and parries.

A reference to Fig. 20, in which the directions of the blade are indicated by means of the hilt and dotted lines, will make it easy for the beginner to place his sword in the seven guarding positions which follow.

Guard One.—Grasp the hilt as shown in Fig. 17, turn the edge to the left with the elbow held close to the body, the wrist well to the front. Let the blade be as nearly as possible parallel to the direction of cut 1, and let it slope in the direction of the target at an angle of about forty-five degrees with the ground: *i.e.* let the point in this, and indeed all the guards, be well advanced to the front.

Guard Two.—Turn the knuckles up, draw the elbow nearer the right side and let the edge face to the right, and let the blade be parallel to cut 2. In this guard the forearm will be more directly pointing towards the target.

Guard Three.—Turn wrist and edge to the left, the hand being rather below the left shoulder, and the blade following the dotted lines marked "third guard."

Guard Four.—Bring the wrist and hand across the body to the right, edge to right and blade following dotted line marked "fourth guard."

Guard Five.—Wrist and edge to the left, with blade pointing vertically downwards.

Guard Six.—Wrist and edge to the right, with blade pointing vertically downwards.

It will be observed that these two guards, five and six, are but extensions of guards three and four, the difference being merely in the height of the hand and inclination of the blade.

Guard Seven.—Raise the hand well above the level of the eyes, so that the target can be seen under the wrist; let the arm be extended, the point of the sword dropped forward to the left and parallel to dotted lines marked "seventh guard," and let the edge face vertically upwards.

It may be here again mentioned that with all guards and parries in actual practice, the "forte," or half nearest the hilt, should be the portion of the blade which meets the opponent's sword when the attack is made.

Left Parry.—Let the wrist be drawn back to within eight or ten inches of the right shoulder, the blade pointing in the direction of the perpendicular line on the target, and let the edge be turned to the right. Now, by a second motion, turn the wrist so that the point drops to the left and forms a circle from left to right and then returns to the former position.

Right Parry.—Drop the point to the rear and form the circle from right to left of your body, the sword returning to its position as before.

Both these circular parries should be learnt and practised for the sake of adding to the strength and suppleness of the wrist; but for actual use it is better to turn the point aside by one of the simple guards, remembering not to let the hand wander far from the line of attack. In other words, you should let your "forte" catch the "foible" of the adversary's blade just sufficiently to turn aside the point, and then instantly give your point or come back to whatever guard you may have assumed in the first instance.

Some diversity of opinion exists as to the best "Engaging Guard" to take up. In the two Figs., 21 and 22, I am inclined to favour the former for use when opposed either to the small sword or the bayonet, and give preference to the latter when facing another broadswordsman. In Fig. 21, it will be observed, the point is well forward, and it is easy with a light pressure to turn aside the opposing point and instantly lunge out in the return. The engagement is here in *tierce*, but it might just as well be in *quarte*, in which case the edge would be turned to the left instead of to the right.

At the same time, the more common engaging guard, the very low hanging guard in Fig. 22, has many merits not possessed by the other. It will be better to constantly practise *both* these guarding

41

FIG. 21.—ENGAGING GUARD, A

positions and then come to a decision as to which you can do best in. Two things are certain, *viz.*, you can, if proficient at both, puzzle an opponent who is at home only in one, and the change of position is a great rest in a long succession of bouts.

It will now be well to combine the cuts and guards, and, for this, take up the second position in front of the target, and in making each cut lunge well out into the third position, not allowing the blade to cut further than the centre of the target. Then spring back to the position from which you lunged and form the guard for the cut you have just made. For instance, having made cut 1 as far as the centre of the target, return to the second position and form guard 1. Similarly for cut 2 and all the other cuts.

In the same way make the points in the lunge, in position three, and the corresponding parries in the second position.

In many works on the subject, the foregoing exercises are given with the return in each case to the first position instead of, as above, to the second. It is, however, advisable to accustom yourself as much as possible to rapid returns from the lunge to the engaging position in which you habitually face an opponent. The change from position one to position three involves a long stretch out, and

FIG. 22.—ENGAGING GUARD, B

the return is, of course, harder than the return to position two, and, for this very reason, it is well to practise the exercises from both initial positions—one and two.

FIG. 23.—POINT, WITH LUNGE

At the risk of being considered old-fashioned, I have given the sword exercise with seven cuts and three points, with corresponding guards and parries, and it is my conviction that the beginner will do well to follow the advice given.

The following instructions are taken from the Manual on the Infantry Sword, now used in the army.

Instructions for Drawing the Sword (Long)

Draw Swords.—Take hold of the scabbard of the sword, with the left hand below the hilt, which should be raised as high as the hip, then bring the right hand smartly across the body, grasping the hilt and turning it at the same time to the rear, raise the hand the height of the elbow, the arm being close to the body.

Two.—Draw the sword from the scabbard, the edge being to the rear, and lower the hand until the upper part of the hilt is opposite the mouth, the blade perpendicular, edge to the left, elbow close to the body, which forms the position "Recover swords."

Three.—Bring the sword smartly down until the hand is in front of the elbow and little finger in line with it, the elbow close to the body, blade perpendicular, edge to the front; which forms the position of "Carry swords;" the left hand resumes the position of "Attention" directly the sword is drawn.

Slope Swords.—Relax the grasp of the last three fingers, and, without disturbing the position of the hand, allow the back of the sword to fall lightly on the shoulder, midway between the neck and the point of the shoulder.

Return Swords.—Carry the hilt to the hollow of the left shoulder (the left hand, as before, raising the scabbard), with the blade perpendicular and the back of the hand to the front, then by a quick turn of the wrist drop the point into the scabbard, turning the edge to the rear until the hand and elbow are in line with each other square across the body.

Two.—Replace the sword in the scabbard, keeping the hand upon the hilt.

Three.—The hands are brought back to the position of "Attention."

Draw Swords.—As before.

Slope Swords.—As before.

Stand at Ease.—Keeping the sword at the "Slope," draw back the right foot six inches, and bend the left knee.

THE FOUR CUTS (FROM SECOND POSITION)

Assault.—Raise the hand and sword to the rear, arm bent, wrist rounded, the back of the sword resting upon the shoulder, with the edge inclined to the right.

One.—Extend the arm, and direct the cut diagonally downwards from right to left, and, continuing the sweep of the sword, prepare for cut "two," the back of the sword upon the left shoulder, edge inclined to the left.

Two.—Cut diagonally downwards from left to right, and turning the wrist let the sword continue its motion until it rests upon the right shoulder, edge to the right.

Three.—Cut horizontally from right to left, and prepare for cut "four," the flat of the sword resting upon the left shoulder.

Four.—Cut horizontally from left to right, and come to the "Engaging Guard" (*vide* Fig. 22).

THE FOUR GUARDS

First.—Raise the hand smartly above the head, and a little in advance of it, the point of the sword lowered to the left front, edge upwards.

Second.—Draw back the elbow to the right, and bring the sword to a diagonal position, covering the right cheek and shoulder, point upwards, inclining to the left, edge to the right.

Third.—Bring the hand across the body towards the left shoulder, edge of the sword to the left, point down and inclining to the front.

Fourth.—Square the upper arm with the shoulder, the

forearm to be in front line with the elbow, and wrist slightly below it, point of the sword inclined to the front, edge to the right.

Engage.—As before.

POINTS AND PARRIES

First.—With a quick motion, direct the point to the front by extending the arm, the arm moving in a straight line to the front of the "First Guard" position, and without altering the direction of the edge.

Parry.—Brace up the arm quickly and parry upwards by forming "First Guard."

Second.—Deliver the point quickly by extending the arm and sword to the front.

Parry.—Draw back the arm and parry to the right, by forming "Second Guard."

Third.—Lowering the point, extend the arm.

Parry.—Draw back the arm, and parry to the left by forming "Third Guard."

Fourth.—Raise the point and deliver the thrust.

Parry.—Parry downwards to the right by forming "Fourth Guard."

It will be worth the reader's while to compare carefully the preceding four cuts and points and their guards and parries, with the earlier exercises, the description of which commences on p. 37.

It will be seen that the third and fifth guards (old style) are merged in one, that the fourth and sixth are also merged in one, and the first guard—the old guard in *quarte*—is dispensed with altogether, and its place taken by a low hanging guard, which is a variation of the old seventh guard, formed with the hand held rather more to the left.

It will also be observed that the parries for the points are also very different. My advice is, "Learn in the old style and then glean all you can from the new."

Extension Motions

It is a good plan to practise the following movements every morning before beginning the sword exercises. To avoid confusion they are here given as in the little Manual on the Infantry Sword; they are effected without any accessories, and you commence by being in the position of "Attention," *i.e.* stand with the heels close together at an angle of about sixty degrees, arms hanging down by the sides, chest expanded, back straight, shoulders back, and head well up.

First Extension Motions

One.—Bring the hands, arms, and shoulders to the front, the fingers lightly touching at the points, nails downwards; then raise them in a circular direction well above the head, the ends of the fingers still touching, the thumbs pointing to the rear, the elbows pressed back and shoulders kept down.

Two.—Separate and extend the arms and fingers upwards, forcing them obliquely back until they are extended on a line with the shoulders, and as they fall gradually from thence to the original position of "Attention," endeavour as much as possible to elevate the neck and chest.

Three.—Turn the palms of the hands to the front, press back the thumbs with the arms extended, and raise them to the rear until they meet above the head, the fingers pointing upwards and the thumbs locked, with the left thumb in front.

Four.—Keep the knees and arms straight, and bend over until the hands touch the feet, the head being brought down in the same direction, and resume the "Third motion" slowly by raising the arms to the front.

Five.—Resume the position of "Attention," as directed in "Second motion."

The whole of these motions should be done very slowly, so as to feel the exertion of the muscles throughout.

47

First Position in Three Motions

One.—Move the hands smartly to the rear, the left grasping the right just above the elbow, and the right supporting the left arm under the elbow.

Two.—Half turn to the left, turning on the heels, so that the back of the left touches the inside of the right heel, the head retaining its position to the front.

Three.—Bring the right heel before the left, the feet at right angles, the right foot pointing to the front.

Second Position on Two Motions

One.—Bend the knees gradually, keeping them as much apart as possible without raising the heels, or changing the erect position of the body.

Two.—Step out smartly with the right foot about eighteen inches in line with the left heel, bringing the foreleg to the perpendicular, and retaining the left as in preceding motion, the weight of the body resting equally upon both legs.

Third Position in One Motion

One.—Step forward to about thirty-six inches, the right knee remaining perpendicular to the instep, the left knee straight and firm, and foot flat upon the ground, the body upright, and the shoulders square to the left.

Loose Practice

In practising with broadswords the blades should be as light as possible, and I believe an eminent firm has brought out a special sword for the purpose. The following rules and suggestions may be of use in independent practice.

1. Helmets, jackets, gauntlets, body pads, and leg pads should invariably be worn.

2. No hits or points to be attempted until the swords have been crossed. The parties should engage out of distance, *i.e.*

after crossing the blades, step back about eight inches and come to the "Engage" *just* out of distance.

3. All cuts and thrusts must be delivered lightly and with the true edge or point. Heavy sweeping cuts should not, under any pretence whatever, or however thickly the parties may be padded, be allowed.

4. Only one cut or thrust should be made on the same lunge.

5. In case the opponents both attack at once, the hit counts to the one in the third position, or on the lunge. If both parties lunge simultaneously, and both bring the hit home at the same instant, no hit is to be scored to either.

6. If one party is disarmed, a hit is scored to his opponent.

7. Care should be taken to protect the inside of the right knee with an extra pad, as this is a particularly tender spot, and a hard hit there may cause serious injury.

When the beginner has established some command over the cutlass he should learn the cavalry sword-exercise, for a description of which the reader is referred to Colonel Bowdler Bell's manual.

CHAPTER 4

Single-Stick

by C. Phillipps-Wolley

Single-stick is to the sabre what the foil is to the rapier, and
while foil-play is the science of using the point only, sabre-play is
the science of using a weapon, which has both point and edge, to
the best advantage. In almost every treatise upon fencing my subject has been treated with scant ceremony. "Fencing" is assumed
to mean the use of the point only, or, perhaps it would not be too
much to say, the use of the foils; whereas fencing means simply (in
English) the art of of-fending another and de-fending yourself with
any weapons, but perhaps especially with all manner of swords.

In France or Spain, from which countries the use of the thrusting-sword was introduced into England, it would be natural enough
to consider fencing as the science of using the point of the sword
only, but here the thrusting-sword is a comparatively modern im-
portation, and is still only a naturalized foreigner, whereas broad-
sword and sabre and single-stick play are older than, and were once
as popular as, boxing. On the other hand, the rapier was in old days
a foreigner of peculiarly shady reputation on these shores, its intro-
ducer being always alluded to in the current literature of that day,
with anathemas, as "that desperate traitour, Rowland Yorke."

"*L'Escrime*" is, no doubt, the national sword-play of France, and,
for Frenchmen, fencing may mean the use of the foil, but broad-
sword and sabre-play are indigenous here, and if fencing is to mean
only one kind of sword-play or sword-exercise, it should mean
single-stick.

Like the swordsmen of India, our gallant forefathers (according to Fuller, in his "Worthies of England") accounted it unmanly to strike below the knee or with the point. But necessity has no laws, still less has it any sense of honour, so that before long English swordsmen realized that the point was much more deadly than the edge, and that, unless they were prepared to be "spitted like cats or rabbits," it was necessary for them either to give up fighting or condescend to learn the new fashion of fence.

As in boxing, it was found that the straight hit from the shoulder came in quicker than the round-arm blow, so in fencing it was found that the thrust got home sooner than the cut, and hence it came that the more deadly style of fighting with the rapier supplanted the old broad-sword play.

Single-stick really combines both styles of fencing. In it the player is taught to use the point whenever he can do so most effectively; but he is also reminded that his sword has an edge, which may on occasion do him good service. It seems, then, to me, that single-stick is the most thoroughly practical form of sword-play for use in those "tight places" where men care nothing for rules, but only want to make the most out of that weapon which the chance of the moment has put into their hands. It may further be said that as the sabre is still supplied to our soldiers, though rarely used for anything more dangerous than a military salute, whereas no one except a French journalist has probably ever seen, what I may be allowed to call, a foil for active service, the science of single-stick has some claim to practical utility even in the nineteenth century, the only sound objection to single-stick being that the sticks used are so light as not to properly represent the sabre.

This is a grave objection to the game, when the game is regarded as representing real business; but for all that, the lessons learnt with the stick are invaluable to the swordsman. The true way to meet the difficulty would be to supplement stick-play by a course with broad-swords, such as are in use in different London gymnasiums, with blunt edges and rounded points.

But gunpowder has taken the place of "cold steel," and arms of precision at a thousand yards have ousted the "white arm" of the chivalrous ages, so that it is really only of single-stick as a sport that men think, if they think of it at all, to-day. As a sport it is second to none of those which can be indulged in in the gymnasium, unless it be boxing; and even boxing has its disadvantages. What the ordinary Englishman wants is a game with which he may fill up the hours during which he cannot play cricket and need not work; a game in which he may exercise those muscles with which good mother Nature meant him to earn his living, but which custom has condemned to rust, while the brain wears out; a game in which he may hurt some one else, is extremely likely to be hurt himself, and is certain to earn an appetite for dinner. If any one tells me that my views of amusement are barbaric or brutal, that no reasonable man ever wants to hurt any one else or to risk his own precious carcase, I accept the charge of brutality, merely remarking that it was the national love of hard knocks which made this little island famous, and I for one do not want to be thought any better than the old folk of England's fighting days.

There is just enough pain about the use of the sticks to make self-control during the use of them a necessity; just enough danger to a sensitive hide to make the game thoroughly English, for no game which puts a strain upon the player's strength and agility only, and none on his nerve, endurance, and temper, should take rank with the best of our national pastimes.

Gallant Lindsey Gordon knew the people he was writing for when he wrote—

No game was ever yet worth a rap,
For a rational man to play,
Into which no accident, no mishap,
Could possibly find its way.

Still, there comes a time, alas! in the lives of all of us, when, though the hand is still ready to smite, the over-worked brain resents the infliction of too many "merry cross-counters," and we cannot afford to go about with black eyes, except as an occasional indulgence. Then it is that single-stick comes in. Boxing is the game of youth, and fencing with foils, we have been assured, improves as men fall into the sere and yellow leaf. Single-stick, then, may be looked upon as a gentle exercise, suitable for early middle age.

There is just enough sting in the ash-plant's kiss, when it catches you on the softer parts of your thigh, your funny bone, or your wrist, to keep you wide awake, and remind you of the good old rule of "grin and bear it;" but the ash-plant leaves no marks which are likely to offend the eyes of squeamish clients or female relations.

Another advantage which single-stick possesses is that you may learn to play fairly well even if you take it up as late in life as at five and twenty; whereas I understand that, though many of my fencing friends were introduced to the foil almost as soon as to the corrective birch, and though their heads are now growing grey, they still consider themselves mere tyros in their art.

That single-stick is a national game of very considerable antiquity, and at one time in great repute on our country greens, no one is likely to deny, nor have I time to argue with them even if I would in this little brochure. Those who are interested in *spadroon*, backsword, and broad-sword will find the subjects very exhaustively treated in such admirable works as Mr. Egerton Castle's "Schools and Masters of Fence." These pages are merely intended for the tyro—they are, at best, a compilation of those notes written during the last ten years in black and white upon my epidermis by the ashplants of Sergeants Waite and Ottaway, and Corporal-Major Blackburn. Two of them, unfortunately, will never handle a stick again, but the last-named is still left, and to him especially I am indebted for anything which may be worth remembering in these pages. A book may teach you the rudiments of any game, but it is only face to face with a *better* player than yourself that you will ever make any real advance in any of the sciences of self-defence.

And here, then, is my first hint, taught by years of experience: If you want to learn to play quickly, if you want to get the most out of your lessons, whether in boxing or stick-play, never encourage your teacher to spare you too much. If you get a stinging crosscounter early in your career as a boxer, which lays you out senseless for thirty seconds, you will find that future antagonists have the greatest possible difficulty in getting home on that spot again. It is the same in single-stick. If you are not spared too much, and are not too securely padded, you will, after the ash-plant has curled once or twice round your thighs, acquire a guard so instinctively accurate, so marvellously quick, that you will yourself be delighted at your cheaply purchased dexterity. The old English players used no pads and no masks, but, instead, took off their coats, and put up their elbows to shield one side of their heads.

There are to-day in England several distinct schools of single-stick, the English navy having, I believe, a school of its own; but all these different schools are separated from one another merely by sets of rules, directing, for the most part, where you may and where you may not hit your adversary.

The best school appears to be that in which all hits are allowed, which might be given by a rough in a street row, or a Sudanese running a-muck. The old trial for teachers of fencing was not a bad test of real excellence in the mastery of their weapon—a fight with three skilled masters of fence (one at a time, of course), then three bouts with valiant unskilled men, and then three bouts against three half-drunken men. A man who could pass this test was a man whose sword could be relied upon to keep his head, and this is what is wanted. All rules, then, which provide artificial protection, as it were—protection other than that afforded by the swordsman's guard—to any part of the body are wrong, and to be avoided.

Let me illustrate my position. I remember well, at Waite's rooms, in Brewer Street, seeing a big Belgian engaged with a gentleman who at that time occupied the honourable position of chopping-block to the rooms. The Belgian had come over to take part in some competition, and was an incomparably better player than the Englishman, but then the Belgian wished to play according to the rules of his own school. It was arranged at last that each should do his worst in his own way, and it was hoped that Providence would take care of the better man.

Unfortunately the worse man of the two had been very much in the habit of taking care of himself when subjected to the attacks of such punishing players as Ottaway and Mr. Jack Angle.

The Belgian's legs had been protected by a rule of fence, which made it illegal to hit below the waist, or some such point, and now naturally they fell an easy prey to the Englishman's ash-plant. The result was, of course, that in a very short time that Belgian's thigh was so wealed that at every feint in that direction he was ready to be drawn, and to uncover head or arm or any well-padded spot, not already sore, to the other man's attack.

Let me touch lightly on one or two little points before plunging *in medias res*. In spite of what I have said about hard hitting, please remember that I have recommended my pupil only to suffer it gladly for his own sake. It will improve his temper and his play. On the other hand, hard, indiscriminate hitting is to be discountenanced for many reasons, and principally because, as a rule, a hard hit means a slow one. Always remember that all the time taken to draw your hand back for a blow is time given to the enemy to get his point in, and that a blow delivered from wrist and arm (bent only as much as it should be when you "engage") would suffice to disable your adversary if the sticks were what they pretend to be, "sharp swords." Again, in ordinary loose play, remember you are playing, or are supposed to be playing, with the weapons of gentlemen, and should show the fine old-fashioned courtesy to one another which is due to a foeman worthy of your steel. If there is a question as to a hit, acknowledge it as against yourself, as in the cut below, by springing up to attention and bringing the hilt up to the level of the mouth, blade upright, and knuckles turned to your front.

FIG. 24.—ACKNOWLEDGING

Again, if you should get an awkward cut, do all you can not to return savagely. If you make any difference at all, play more lightly for the next five minutes, otherwise you may drift into a clumsy slogging match, ending in bad blood. Finally, if you do get hold of a vicious opponent, do not, whatever you do, show that you mind his blows. If he sees that a cut at a particular place makes you flinch, he will keep on feinting at it until he hits you wherever he pleases; but if, on the contrary, you take no notice of punishment, you are apt to dishearten the adversary, who feels that your blows hurt him, and is uncertain whether his tell upon you in like manner. I may as well say here that throughout this paper, I have, as far as possible, used English words to explain my meaning, abstaining from the French terms of the fencing school, as being likely to confuse a beginner, who may not want to learn French as an introduction to fencing.

OUTFIT

The accessories necessary for single-stick are much more numerous now than in the old days on the village green. Then two stout ash-plants, and the old North-country prayer (beautifully terse), *"God, spare our eyes!"* were considered all that was necessary. Now a complete equipment costs rather more than a five-pound note.

First, then, there is the helmet, constructed more solidly than that used for foil play, although the wire mesh of which it is made is generally a good deal wider than the mesh of the fencing mask. The best helmet is made of stout wire, with a top of buffalo hide, completely covering the head, and with padded ear-pieces to take off the effect of a slashing cut. These are better than those made of cane, which are apt to give way before a stout thrust and let in the enemy's point to the detriment of eyes and complexion. Be careful, in choosing your helmet, to see that it fits you exactly, as a nodding helm may, in a close thing, so interfere with your sight as to give your adversary a very considerable advantage. The jacket generally used for this play is made like a pea-jacket, with two sleeves, and should be of stout leather. If this is loose fitting, it will afford ample protection, and is not so hot as the padded coat sometimes seen. Besides being too hot, the handsome white kid padded jackets soon get holes made in them by the ash-plant, whereas the brown leather is seldom torn.

In addition to the jacket, an apron of leather, extending from the waist almost to the knee, should be worn, covering both thighs, and saving the wearer from dangerously low hits.

Some men wear a cricket pad on the right leg. This, I think, makes a man slow on his feet, and is besides unnecessary. The calf of any one in condition should be able to despise ash-plants; and, as I said before, a bare leg makes you wonderfully quick with your low guards.

Stick play is a fine test of a man's condition. At first every hit leaves an ugly mark, but as soon as the player gets really "fit," it takes a very heavy blow indeed to bruise him. The sticks themselves should be ash-plants, about forty inches in length and as thick as a man's thumb, without knots and unpeeled.

If you want them to last any time it is as well to keep a trough of water in the gymnasium, and leave your ash-plants to soak in it until they are wanted. If you omit to do this, two eager players, in half an hour's loose play, will destroy half a dozen sticks, which adds considerably to the cost of the amusement.

The old English sword hilt was a mere cross-piece; but in play it has always been customary to protect the fingers with a basket. This may be either of wicker or of buffalo hide. The latter is infinitely the best, as wearing much longer, affording a better protection to the fingers, and not scraping the skin off the knuckles as the wicker-baskets too often do. The basket has a hole on either side; one close to the rim, and the other about a couple of inches from the edge. In putting your basket on, put your stick through the former first, as otherwise you will not be able to get a grip of your stick or any room for the play of your wrist.

There is only one other thing necessary, and then you may consider yourself safe as a schoolboy with the seat of his trousers full of the dormitory towels: and that is either a stout elastic ring round your wrist—a ring as thick as your thumb—or a good long gauntlet. I rather recommend the ring as interfering less with the freedom of your hand, and as protecting more effectually that weak spot in your wrist where the big veins are. If a blow catches you squarely across this spot, when it is unprotected, you may expect your right hand to lose its cunning for a good many minutes. By the way, it is as well to see that the collar of your jacket is sufficiently high and well supplied with buttons, otherwise there is apt to be a dangerous gap between the shoulder and the bottom of the helmet.

One last word: if you see that the point of your stick is broken, don't go on playing; stop at once. A split ash-plant is as dangerous as a buttonless foil, and just as likely as not to go through the meshes of a mask, and blind where you only meant to score. As the chief fault of single-stick as a training for the use of the sabre is that the stick does not properly represent the weight of the weapon which it simulates, it is not a bad thing to accustom yourself to using the heaviest sticks in the gymnasium. This will strengthen your wrist, and when in a competition you get hold of a light ash-plant, you will be all the quicker for your practice with a heavier stick.

A cut earlier in this book by Mr. Graham Simpson represents the way to acknowledge a hit, and a cut by the same artist a few pages later illustrates, as far as we know it, the less careful method of our forefathers. The use of the elbow to shield the head, though common in the contests on the village greens, was in its way no doubt more foolish than our pads; for though a sturdy yokel might take a severe blow from a cudgel on his bare arm, without wincing, the toughest arm in England would have had no chance against a sabre.

POSITION

Having now secured the necessary implements, let us begin to learn how to use them. First, as to the stick, which, you will remember, represents for the present a sabre, and consequently a weapon of which one edge only is sharpened. In order that every blow dealt with the stick should be dealt with what represents the sharp or "true" edge of the sword, it is only necessary to see that you get a proper grip of your weapon in the first instance. To do this shut your fingers round the hilt, and straighten your thumb along the back of the hilt, thus bringing your middle knuckles (or second joints of your fingers) and the true edge into the same line. If you keep this grip you may rest assured that every blow you deal will be with the edge.

And now as to position—the first position from which eve-

FIG. 25.—OLD STYLE

ry attack, feint, or guard, begins. Ned Donelly, the great boxer, used to tell his pupils that if a man knew how to use his feet, his hands would take care of themselves. And what is undoubtedly true in boxing is equally true in fencing. "Look that your foundations are sure" should be every fighting man's motto. Take trouble, then, about the position of the feet from the first. To come on to the engaging guard, as shown in Fig. 26, stand upright, your heels together, your feet at right angles to one another, your right foot pointing to your front, your left foot to your left, your stick in your right hand, loosely grasped and sloped over your right shoulder, your right elbow against your side, and your right hand about on a level with it, your left hand behind your back, out of harm's way.

It is not a bad plan to put the fingers of the left hand through the belt at the back of the waist. If this is done, it counteracts, to a certain extent, that tendency to bring the left hand in front, which a good many beginners display, and for which they get punished by many an unpleasant rap on the knuckles.

Now take a short pace to the front with the right foot, and, in

FIG. 26.—ENGAGING GUARD

the words of the instructor, "sit down," *i.e.* bend both legs at the knee, so that the calves are almost at right angles to the thighs. This position will be found a severe strain upon the muscles at first, but they will soon get used to it. The object of the position is twofold. First, the muscles are thus coiled, as it were, ready for a spring at the shortest notice; and in the second place, the surface which your stick has to guard is thus considerably reduced. Be careful to keep the right heel in a line with the left heel, a space equal to about twice the length of your own foot intervening between them, and see that your right toe points squarely to the front and your left toe to your left. If your right toe is turned in, you will never advance straight to your front; and if your left toe is turned in, you contract the base upon which your body rests, and very soon will begin to roll and lose your balance altogether. As far as the legs and feet are concerned you are now in your proper position, which you will only leave when you lunge, or when you straighten yourself to acknowledge a hit, and to which you will invariably return as soon as you engage.

If you wish to advance, advance the right foot a short pace, bringing the left after it at once, so that the two resume their relative positions to one another, half a pace nearer your enemy. If you wish to retire, reverse this movement, retiring with the left foot and following it with the right. In both cases keep your eyes to the front, your feet at right angles, and your knees bent.

Now as to the stick. There are two forms of guard in common use amongst players, the hanging and the upright guard, of both of which illustrations will be found in these pages. In Rowland Yorke's time men sought for what I think they called "the universal parry" almost as anxiously as they did for the alchemist's stone which should turn all things to gold. Of course such a thing has never been found, but either of these guards, if truly taken and *kept*, will stop the attacks of most men as long as you keep them at their proper distance.

In passing, let me say that if a man *will* try to overwhelm you with rushes, the best thing you can do is to straighten your stick, thrust, and *don't let the stick run through the basket.* This has a wonderfully soothing effect upon an excitable player.

In Fig. 27 the upright guard (or high *tierce*) is shown, in which the right elbow should be close in to the side, the forearm at right angles to the body, wrist bent, so as to turn the knuckles outwards, and the stick pointed upwards, at an angle of about 45°. In Fig. 26, the hanging guard, the point of the stick should be inclined slightly downwards, the knuckles turned upwards, the forearm should be kept slightly bent, the hilt a little outside the right knee, the point of the stick a little low and in the direction of the left front.

If the point of the stick be kept up, the adversary finds a way in by cutting upwards under the point; if the hilt is not outside the right knee, the back of the sword arm will be unprotected; and if the sword arm itself is not kept slightly bent, no effective blow can be delivered by it without first drawing back the hand.

This, of course, is a fatal fault. The moment your adversary sees your hand go back, he will come out. As you retire for the spring, he will spring. *Time* is the very essence of single-stick, and the chief object of the player should be to make his attack in the fewest possible motions. For this reason a slightly bent arm

FIG. 27.—UPRIGHT GUARD, OR HIGH TIERCE

is necessary when on guard. Of course if the arm is unduly bent the elbow will be exposed, but a little practice will soon enable any moderately supple man to so hold his arm as to be ready to cut direct from his guard and yet keep his elbow out of peril. And this brings me to a question often discussed amongst players, *viz.* which is the better guard, the upright or the hanging guard, for general purposes. Although I have been taught to use the hanging guard myself ever since I began to play, I unhesitatingly say that the upright guard is the better one, as enabling a player to save time in the attack. In the hanging guard the knuckles (*i.e.* the edge) are up and away from the enemy; the wrist must be turned before the edge can be brought into contact with his body, and this takes time, however little. In the upright guard the knuckles (*i.e.* the edge) are towards your opponent, the arm is ready flexed, everything is in readiness for the blow. If, then, as I believe, the advantages of the two guards, as guards, are equal, the advantage of the upright guard as a position to attack from seems to me undeniable.

In all guards remember that it is not sufficient to oppose some part of your weapon to your adversary's. You must meet him, if possible, with what the old masters called the "forte" of your blade, that is, the part from the hilt to the middle of the sword, with which you have naturally more power of resistance than with the lower half of the blade. Of course all guards must be made with the edge of the sword outwards, and make sure that you really *feel* your enemy's blade (*i.e.* make a good clean guard) before attempting to return his attack.

There is another matter to which many teachers pay too little attention, but which is as important as any point in the fencer's art. It is obvious that the player should try, if possible, to hit without being hit. To do this effectively it is necessary in attacking to maintain what fencers call a good "opposition," that is to say, to so carry your stick in cutting or thrusting at him as to protect yourself in the line in which you are attacking.

This is easier to explain in practice than on paper, but it may perhaps be sufficiently explained by examples. If, for instance, you are cutting at the left side of your opponent's head, you must, to stop a possible counter from him, keep your hilt almost as high as the top of your own head and carry your hand well across to your own left. If you do this correctly, you will, in case he should cut at your left cheek as you cut at his, stop his cut with the upper part of your stick.

Again, in thrusting at him, if you keep your hand as high as your shoulder, and in a line with your right shoulder, you will protect the upper half of your own body from a counter, so that, even if your thrust fails and does not get home, the upper part of your blade will stop his cut.

It is necessary to study so to attack your opponent that, in the very act of delivering a cut or thrust, you may stop him in as many lines or directions of attack as possible.

If you find your man will counter in spite of all that you can do, take advantage of this habit of his by feinting a cut to draw his counter, stop this, and return.

This will have the effect of making him do the leading, which will be all in your favour.

Hits, Guards, Feints, Etc.

For the purposes of instruction and description, the principal hits in single-stick have been numbered and described according to the parts of the body at which they are aimed.

There are four principal hits: (1) a cut at your opponent's left cheek; (2) a cut at his right cheek; (3) a cut at his left ribs; (4) a cut at his right ribs. 5 and 6 are mere repetitions of 3 and 4 on a lower level, guarded in the same way, and aimed at the inside and outside of the right leg instead of at the ribs.

In the accompanying cuts numbered 28, 29, 30, 31, the four principal attacks and the stops for them have been illustrated, and with their help and a long looking-glass in front of him the young player ought to be able to put himself into fairly good position.

In addition to the cuts there is the point, which, as our forefathers discovered, is far more deadly than the edge. Of this more later on. Almost every cut is executed upon the lunge. As you and your adversary engage, you are practically out of each other's range unless you lunge.

Standing in the first position the heels are two feet apart. On the lunge, I have seen Corporal-Major Blackburn, a man, it is true, over six feet in height, measure, from his left heel to a point on the floor, level with his sword point, nearly ten feet. This gives some idea of what is to be expected from a man who can lunge properly. To do this, throw out the right foot as far as it will go to the front, keeping the heels still in line and the right foot straight.

Keep the outside edge of the left foot firmly down upon the floor, and keep it still at right angles to the right foot. If your left foot begins to leave the ground you have over-reached yourself; you will find it impossible to get back, and you will be at your opponent's mercy. See that your right knee is exactly over your right ankle, your left leg straight, your chest square to the front, and your head well up. If you can get yourself into this position, you will have no difficulty in recovering yourself if your lunge fails, and you will gain nothing by bending your body forward from the waist. On the contrary, you will spoil your balance.

This lunge will do for every cut and every point.

To recover after a lunge, throw your weight well back upon your left leg, and use the muscles of the right thigh and calf to

FIG. 28.—CUT 1 AND GUARD

FIG. 29.—CUT 2 AND GUARD

shoot yourself back into position. If the knee of the right leg has been kept exactly over the ankle, the impetus necessary to regain your original position will be easily obtained. If, however, the right foot has been protruded too far, and the caution as to the knee and ankle disregarded, you will find yourself unable to return quickly from the lunging position, and will consequently be at your opponent's mercy. It is in the operation of returning from the lunge that the player realizes to the full the advantage of keeping the shoulders well back and head erect.

The illustrations should speak for themselves, but perhaps I had better explain them.

In cut 1 (Fig. 28), lunge out and cut at the left cheek of your opponent, straightening the arm and turning the knuckles down.

To stop this cut, raise the engaging guard (hanging guard, Fig. 26) slightly, and bring the hand somewhat nearer the head, as shown in the illustration, or stop it with the upright guard, with the elbow kept well in and the right hand about on a level with the left shoulder.

FIG. 30.—CUT 3 AND GUARD

FIG. 31.—CUT 4 AND GUARD

In cut 2 (Fig. 29), lunge out and cut at your opponent's right cheek, with your arm straight and knuckles up. The natural guard for this is the high upright guard, with the elbow well in to the right side, the arm bent and turned slightly outwards, and wrist and knuckles turned well to the right.

In cut 3 (Fig. 30), make free use of the wrist, bringing your blade round in the smallest space possible, and come in on your man's ribs with your arm straight and knuckles turned downwards.

To stop this cut you may either use a low hanging guard, brought across to the left side, the right hand about on a level with the left shoulder, or a low upright guard, with the hilt just outside the left thigh.

The hanging guard is the safer one of the two, as it is difficult in practice to get low enough with the hilt in the upright guard to stop a low cut of this kind.

In cut 4 (Fig. 31), cut at your adversary's right ribs, and keep your knuckles up, and when he attacks you on this line, stop him with the hanging guard held low on your right side, or with the upright guard, with arm, wrist, and knuckles turned outwards.

Cuts 5 and 6 are made like cuts 3 and 4 respectively, and must be met in all cases by a low hanging guard. It is well to practise these low hanging guards continually, as a man's legs are perhaps the most exposed part of his body.

The point when used is given by a simple straightening of the arm on the lunge, the knuckles being kept upwards, and, in ordinary play, the grip on the stick loosened, in order that it may run freely through the hilt, and thus save your opponent from an ugly bruise, a torn jacket, or possibly a broken rib. When the knuckles are kept up in giving point, the sword hand should be opposite the right shoulder. But the point may also be delivered with the knuckles down, in which case the hand should be opposite to the left shoulder.

The point may be parried with any of the guards previously described.

It is well to remember that one of the most effective returns which can be made from any guard is a point, and that a point can be made certainly from every hanging guard by merely straightening the arm from the guard, lunging, and coming in under your

FIG. 32.—THE POINT

opponent's weapon. But perhaps this is a thing to be learnt rather from practical play than from a book.

Now, it is obvious that if any of the foregoing guards are as good as they have been described, it is necessary to induce your adversary to abandon them if you are ever to score a point.

This may be done in a variety of ways, when you have assured yourself that he is invulnerable to a direct attack, not to be flurried by a fierce onslaught, or slow enough to let you score a "remise"—that is, a second hit—the first having been parried, but not returned.

The first ruse to adopt, of course, is the feint—a feint being a false attack, or rather a move as if to attack in a line which you threaten, but in which you do not intend to attack. All feints should be *strongly pronounced* or clearly shown. A half-hearted feint is worse than useless; it is dangerous. If you have a foeman worthy of your steel facing you, he will detect the fraud at once, and use the time wasted by you over a feeble feint to put in a time thrust.

The ordinary feint is made by an extension of the arm as if to cut without moving the foot to lunge, the lunge being made the moment you have drawn off your enemy's guard and laid bare the real object of your attack.

Sometimes, however, if you cannot succeed otherwise, a half or short lunge for your feint, to be turned into a full lunge as you

FIG. 33.—A RUSE

see your opening, may be found a very useful variation of the
ordinary feint. If you find feints useless, you may try to compass
your adversary's downfall by "a draw." All the time that you are
playing you should try to be using your head, to be thinking out
your plans and trying to discover his. In nine cases out of ten he
has some favourite form of attack. If you discover what it is, and
know how to stop it, indulge him, and invite him even to make
it, having previously formed some little scheme of attack of your
own upon this opening. Let me illustrate my meaning by examples. If you notice a hungry eye fixed yearningly on your tender
calf, let your calf stray ever so little from under the protection of
the hanging guard. If this bait takes your friend in, and he comes
with a reckless lunge at it, throwing all his heart into the cut,
spring up to your full height, heels together, and leg well out of
danger, and gently let your avenging rod fall along his spine. This,
by the way, is the only occasion, except when you are acknowl-
edging a hit, on which you may be allowed to desert the first
position for legs and feet.

But this is a very old ruse, and most players know it: a much
better one may be founded upon it. If, for instance, you think you
detect any coquettish symptoms in the right leg of your adversary,
you may know at once what he is meditating. Oblige him at once.
Lunge freely out at his leg, which will of course be at once with-
drawn. This, however, you were expecting, and as his leg goes back
your hand goes up to the high hanging guard, covering your head

from his cut. This cut stopped, he is at your mercy, and you may cut him in halves or crimp his thigh at your leisure. This position is illustrated in Fig. 33.

Once again: some men set their whole hearts on your sleeve, and you may, if yours is the hanging guard, lure them to their destruction through this lust of theirs. Gradually, as the play goes on, your arm tires, your hand sinks, your arm at last is bare, and the enemy comes in with a cut which would almost lay open the gauntlet, were it not that at that moment you come to the low upright guard and return at his left cheek. These are what are known as draws, and their number is unlimited.

Another thing sometimes heard of in single-stick play is "a gain." This is a ruse for deceiving your opponent as to distance, and is achieved by bringing the left heel up to the right, in the course of the play, without abandoning the normal crouching position. This, of course, makes your lunge two feet longer than your victim has any reason for believing it to be.

A false beat is another very common form of attack, consisting of a cut aimed at the hilt or at the forte of your stick, the object being to make you raise your point, if possible, so that the attacker may come in under with cut three.

This is very well met by a thrust, the arm being merely straightened from the guard, and the lunge delivered directly the "beat" is made.

A pretty feint having the same effect as the "beat," as opening up cut three, is a long feint with the point at the chest, cut three being given as the sword rises to parry the point.

But probably I have already transgressed the limits of my paper. What remains to be taught, and I know full well that it is everything except the merest rudiments, must be learned stick in hand. I can only wish the beginner luck, and envy him every hour which he is able to devote to acquiring a knowledge of sword-play.

THE SALUTE

Although the salute is a mere piece of sword drill, of no use for practical purposes, it is still worth learning, as being the preliminary flourish common at all assaults-at-arms, and valuable in itself as reminding the players that they are engaged in a knightly game, and one which insists on the display of the greatest courtesy by one opponent to the other. Even if you are playing with bare steel, it is expected of you that you should kill your enemy like a knight, and not like a butcher; much more then, when you are only playing a friendly bout with him, should you show him all possible politeness. On entering the ring you should have all your harness on except your mask; this you should carry in your left hand until you are face to face with your antagonist. When in the ring, lay your helmet down on your left hand and come to the slope swords—your blade upon your right shoulder, your elbow against your side and your hilt in a line with your elbow, your knuckles outwards. Your body should be erect, your head up, your heels together, your right foot pointing straight to your front, your left foot at right angles to it pointing to the left.

Both men acting together now come to the engaging guard, and beat twice, stick against stick; they then come back to the "recover" by bringing the right foot back to the left, and bringing the stick into an upright position in front of the face, basket outwards, and thumb on a level with the mouth.

After a slight pause, salute to the left in *quarte, i.e.* extend the stick to your left front across the body, keeping the elbow fairly close to the side and the finger-nails upwards; then pause again for a second, and salute to the right in *tierce* (the back of the hand up); pause again, and salute to the front, by extending the arm in that direction, the point of the stick towards your left front. Now step forward about two feet with the right foot and come to the engaging guard, beat twice, draw the left foot up to the right, draw yourself up to your full height, and come again to the recover, drop your stick to the second guard (*i.e.* low hanging guard for the outside of the leg), making a slight inclination of the body at the same time (probably this is meant for a bow ceremonious), and then you may consider yourself at liberty to put on your mask and begin.

Don't forget, when you cross sticks, to step out of distance again at once. This salute, of course, is only usual at assaults-at-arms, which are modern tournaments arranged for the display of the men's skill and the entertainment of their friends. At the assault-at-arms, as we understand it generally, there is no element of competition, there are no prizes to be played for, and therefore, so long as a good display is made, every one is satisfied, and nobody cares who gets the most points in any particular bout.

In competitions this is not so, and time is an object; so that as soon as the men can be got into the ring they are told to put their masks on and begin.

In assaults and in general play you cannot be too careful to acknowledge your adversary's hits. In a competition do nothing of the kind. The judges will see that every point made is scored, and you may safely relieve your mind from any anxiety on that ground. But in general play it is different, and you cannot be too careful in scoring your adversary's points, or be too liberal in allowing them, even if some of them are a little bit questionable.

ACKNOWLEDGING

The ordinary form of acknowledgment (and a very graceful one it is) is accomplished as follows:—On being hit, spring to attention, with your heels together and body erect, at the same time bringing your sword to the recover, *i.e.* sword upright in front of your face, thumb in a line with your mouth, and knuckles outwards.

The acknowledgment should be only a matter of seconds, and when made the player should come back to the engaging guard and continue the bout.

FOUL HITS

Of course there are occasions on which the best player cannot help dealing a foul hit. When this happens there is nothing to be done except to apologize; but most of these hits may be avoided by a little care and command of temper. By a foul hit is meant a blow dealt to your opponent on receiving a blow from him—a hit given, not as an attempt to "time," but instead of a guard and, as a matter of fact, given very often on the "blow for blow" principle.

This, of course, is great nonsense, if you assume, as you should do, that the weapons are sharp, when such exchanges would be a little more severe than even the veriest glutton for punishment would care for.

If you only want to see who can stand most hammering with

an ash-plant, then your pads are a mistake and a waste of time. Ten minutes without them will do more to settle that question than an hour with them on.

There ought to be some way of penalizing the player who, after receiving a palpable hit himself, fails to acknowledge it, and seizes the opportunity instead to strike the hardest blow he is able to at the unprotected shoulder or arm of his adversary.

One more word and we have done with the courtesies of sword-play.

Don't make any remarks either in a competition (this, of course, is worst of all) or in an ordinary bout. Don't argue, except with the sticks. Remember that the *beau-ideal* swordsman is one who fights hard, with "silent lips and striking hand."

COMPETITIONS

Once a man has mastered the rudiments of any game and acquired some considerable amount of dexterity in "loose play," he begins to long to be pitted against some one else in order to measure his strength. Before long the limits of his own gymnasium grow too small for his ambition, and then it is that we may expect to find him looking round for a chance of earning substantial laurels in public competitions. Unfortunately the stick-player will not find many opportunities of displaying his skill in public. As far as the present writer knows, there are only two prizes offered annually in London for single-stick, and neither of these attract much attention. One of them is given at the Military Tournament at Islington, in June, and one at the German Gymnasium, in December. The former of these prizes is open only to soldiers, militia-men, or volunteers, the latter to any member of a respectable athletic club, who is prepared to pay 2/6d. for his entrance fee. The attendance of spectators at both shows is very poor, which is to be regretted, as the interest of the public in any game generally goes a long way towards insuring improvement in the play.

It is just as well, before entering for either of these competitions, to know something about the conditions under which they take place, and the rules which govern them. The bouts are generally played in a fourteen foot ring, at least that is the statement in the notice to players, and it is as well to be prepared to confine your movements to such a limited area. As a matter of fact, no objection ever seems to be raised to a competitor who transgresses this rule, and we remember to have seen a nimble player skipping about like an electrified eel outside the magic circle, until stopped by a barrier of chairs at the edge of the big arena.

At the Military Tournament the play is for the best out of three hits, *i.e.* the man who scores the first two points wins. At the German Gymnasium the competitor who first scores five wins the bout. This is better than at the Tournament, although it will seem to some that even this is hardly a sufficient test of the merits of each player. The bouts seem too short, but probably this is unavoidable; that which is to be regretted and might be remedied, being that no points are given for "form:" the result is that, in many cases, the anxiety to score the necessary points as soon as possible results in very ugly and unscientific rushes, in which no guards are attempted and from which the most reckless and rapid hitter comes out the winner. This, of course, is the same for every one, and therefore perfectly fair, but it does not tend to elevate the style of play.

But the great difficulty at these competitions appears to be the difficulty of judging. And here let me say at once that it is as far from my intention to find fault with any individual judge as it possibly can be. Being English, I believe them to be above suspicion; being sometimes a competitor myself, it would not be for me to impugn their honesty if they were not. Whatever he does, I would always advise the athlete to preserve his faith in judges and a stoical silence when he does not quite agree with them.

All I would suggest for the benefit of judges and judged alike in these trials of skill which test the eyesight and quickness of the umpires almost as much as the eyesight and quickness of the competitors, is that some definite code of scoring should be established and recognized amongst the different schools-of-arms in England.

In order to facilitate the scoring they have a very good plan at the Military Tournament of chalking the competitors' sticks. This precaution ensures a mark upon the jacket every time the ash-plant hits it; but even this is not always sufficient, for it is quite possible for a true guard to be opposed to a hard cut with a pliant stick, with the result that the attacker's stick whips over and leaves a mark which ought not to be scored, for had the weapons been of steel this could not have happened.

This, however, is a point which would generally be detected by one of the three judges in the ring.

What gives rise to question in players' minds is not any small point like this, so much as the question of timing and countering.

To take the last first: If A and B lunge together, both making direct attacks, and both get home simultaneously, it is generally admitted that the result is a counter, and nothing is to be scored to any one.

But if A makes a direct attack, and B, ignoring it, stands fast and counters, this is a wilful omission to protect himself on his part; and even if his cut should get home as soon as A's it should not count, nor, I think, should it be allowed to cancel A's point, for A led, as the movement of his foot in lunging showed, and B's plain duty was to stop A's attack before returning it. This he would have done naturally enough if he had had the fear of a sharp edge before his eyes.

I even doubt whether a time-thrust or cut should ever be allowed to score, unless the result of it be such as would have rendered the direct attack ineffectual in real fighting. Should not the rule be, either that the point scores to the person making the direct attack, as shown by the action of his foot in lunging (unless, indeed, the attacked person has guarded and returned, when, of course, the point is his), or else make the rule a harder one, but equally fair for every one, and say no hits shall count except those made clean without a counter, *i.e.* to score a point the player must hit his adversary without being hit himself?

Of course bouts would take longer to finish if this were the rule, but such a rule would greatly simplify matters.

The really expert swordsman is surely he who inflicts injuries without receiving any, not he who is content to get rather the best of an exchange of cuts, the least of which would with sharp steel put any man *hors de combat*.

In connection with public competitions, I may as well warn the tyro against what is called "a surprise." On entering the ring the men face each other, come on the engaging guard, and begin at the judge's word of command. The sticks must have been fairly crossed before hits may be counted. But it is as well the moment your stick has crossed your opponent's to step out of distance again, by taking a short pace to the rear with the left foot and bringing the right foot, after it. You can always come in again at short notice; but if you do not keep a sharp look out, a very alert opponent may cross swords with you and tap you on the arm almost in the same movement. If he does you may think it rather sharp practice, but you will find that it scores one to him nevertheless. As no word of practical advice founded on experience should be valueless, let me add one here to would-be competitors. Do not rely upon other people for masks, aprons, or other necessaries of the game. You cannot expect a gymnasium to which you do not belong to furnish such things for you, and even if they were provided they probably would not fit you. Bring all you want for yourself; and if you value your own comfort or personal appearance when you leave the scene of the competition, let your bag, on arriving, contain towels, brushes, and such other simple toilet necessaries as you are likely to require.

CHAPTER 5

The Bayonet

History tells us that firearms of sorts were in existence as far back as the fourteenth century, and that they were probably of Flemish origin. Certain it is that, prior to 1500, there were large bodies of troops armed with what may be called portable *culverins*, and in 1485 the English yeomen of the guard were armed with these clumsy weapons. Later on, in the middle of the sixteenth century, we hear of the long-barrelled *harquebus* being used in Spain, and before the close of the century the *muschite* was in use in the English army. This was a heavier weapon than the harquebus, and the soldiers were provided with a long spiked stake with a fork at the upper end in which to rest the ponderous barrel whilst they took aim.

The method of discharging these weapons was primitive in the extreme, as it was necessary to hold a lighted match to the priming, in a pan at the right side of the barrel, and one can imagine what a lot of fizzing, spluttering, and swearing there must have been in damp weather!

Improvements in the *harquebus* and *musket*, as it got to be called later on, continued to be developed from time to time. In the early days, matchlocks were sneered at as being inferior to cross-bows, much in the same way that the first railway engine was contemptuously spoken of and written about by the coaching men at the beginning of this century; but when in 1700 the flint-lock musket made its appearance popular prejudice was shaken, and it was completely removed in 1820 when percussion guns came into pretty general use.

This may appear to be a digression and somewhat outside the scope of this little work. I give it, however, to show the origin of the rifle, to which, after all, the bayonet is but an adjunct.

About the middle of the seventeenth century it occurred to the sapient mind of one Puséygur, a native of Bayonne, in France, that it would be a grand thing to have a sharp point on which to receive an advancing adversary after one had missed him, or the fizzling matchlock had failed to go off. The weapon devised was a sharp-bladed knife, about eighteen inches long, with a rounded handle six or eight inches long, to fit like a plug into the muzzle of the musket, and the bayonet in this form was used in England and France about the year 1675. It was, of course, impossible to fire the piece with the bayonet fixed; it was a case of fire first and then fix bayonets with all possible dispatch. One can imagine what receiving a cavalry charge must have meant in those days. Towards the close of the seventeenth century an important step was made in the right direction. Bayonets were then for the first time attached to the barrel by two rings, by which means the gun could be fired whilst the bayonet was in its place and ready for instant use. Very early in the eighteenth century a further improvement was invented, in the shape of a socketed bayonet, which was firmer and more satisfactory than anything previously devised.

The British bayonet in the hands of our soldiers has over and over again carried victory into the serried ranks of our adversaries, but, now that arms of precision have reached such a pitch of perfection, and are still on the advance in the matter of rapid firing, it is to be doubted whether hand-to-hand conflicts will play a very prominent part in the battles of the future.

A distinction must be drawn between the ordinary weapon with which the Guards and army generally were till recently provided (I refer to the triangular-fluted bayonet, used exclusively for thrusting purposes), and the sword-bayonet, which serves both for cutting and thrusting. The advantage of the former was evidently its lightness and handiness; but it must be remembered that, save for thrusting, spiking a gun, or boring a hole in a leather strap, it was practically useless, whereas the sharp edge of the sword-bayonet makes it an excellent companion to Tommy Atkins on all sorts of occasions, too numerous to mention.

In the early months of the present year the new rifle and bayonet placed in the hands of the Guards caused a good deal of comment. As my readers are aware, the new arm is a magazine small-bore rifle, carrying a long conical ball. It is not a pretty-looking weapon, and its serviceable qualities have yet to be tested in actual warfare. But it is with the bayonet we are now chiefly concerned. At first sight it reminds one of an extra strong sardine-box opener, but on closer inspection it is evident that, though quite capable of dealing with tinned-meat cans, etc., it has very many merits which are wanting in all the other bayonets which have gone before it. It is a strong double-edged, sharp-pointed knife, twelve inches long, rather more than an inch wide, and about a fifth of an inch deep through the strong ridge which runs down the centre of the blade from point to hilt. The handle is of wood, and it is fastened to the muzzle of the rifle by means of a ring and strong spring catch or clip. Altogether it is almost a model of the early Roman sword.

From this short description it will be seen that, though the soldier loses a good many inches in reach, he is provided with an excellent hunting-knife, which can be turned to any of the uses of a knife—from slaughtering a foe to cutting up tobacco.

Then, again, it is possible that the loss in actual reach may be more than compensated for at very close quarters by the greater ease with which a man can "shorten arms" effectively as well as by the double edge. Every ounce saved in the weight of a soldier's accoutrements is a great gain, and these new bayonets are light and, as I have hinted, are likely to be extremely useful for the every-day work of a long march.

It is not my intention to deal with the bayonet-exercise as practised by squads of infantry, but, before proceeding to deal with some of the more important situations in attack and defence, I would advise those who wish to become proficient to learn the drill. The best way to do this is to join the Volunteers, and get all the squad work possible as a means of gaining a *command* over the weapon—the continued use of which for any length of time is extremely fatiguing. When the rudiments are mastered, and you know fairly well how to respond to the reiterated words of command: "High Guard"—"Point;" "Low Guard"—"Point," etc., and can form the "pints" and guards in a respectable manner, it will be well to join some school of arms with a proficient and painstaking military instructor who is also an expert swordsman. I say *swordsman* advisedly, because I am convinced that it is only one who is a fencer who can be really qualified to impart knowledge on the subject of weapons chiefly used for pointing.

No man can be said to use the bayonet efficiently who is not able to tackle another man similarly armed—a swordsman on foot or a mounted man armed with the cavalry sabre.

For ordinary practice the first thing to be secured is a good spring-bayonet musket, somewhere about the weight of the ordinary rifle, provided with a bayonet which, by means of a strong spiral spring inside the barrel, can be pressed back eighteen inches or so when it comes in contact with the object thrust against. It is hardly necessary to observe that the point of the bayonet must be covered with a good button, similar to those used on fencing foils, only much larger. The button should be tightly encased with layer upon layer of soft leather, and then bound over with stout parchment or stiff leather, and tied very strongly with whipcord or silk just behind the button. This precaution is very necessary to guard against broken ribs, collar-bones, etc.

The illustrations which embellish or disfigure this chapter do not profess to do more than indicate a few of the more important positions, points, and guards which occur in bayonet-exercise: for fuller details the reader is referred to the various manuals issued from time to time by the Horse Guards and War Office authorities. In these little books will be found all the words of command and, I believe, illustrations of every point and parry.

At an assault, and opposed to a man armed also with a bayonet, the first position is indicated by the accompanying sketch. The head should be held well up, the chest expanded, and the weight of the body nearly evenly balanced on both feet, which should be about eighteen or twenty inches apart, so as to give a good firm base without detracting from the rapidity of advance and retreat. In the case of a tall man, the feet will be rather further apart than with a short man; but this is a matter which can be easily adjusted to suit the requirements of each particular case.

The great thing is to get accustomed to the position—to feel

FIG. 34.—ON GUARD

FIG. 35.—POINT, FROM GUARD

"at home" in it—and to be able to shift it at a moment's notice, and, when necessary, to make a firm stand. The drill work is very good for all this, and though it is tedious and irritating to many, it is worth what it costs.

In Fig. 35 we have the point from guard, and in delivering this point the feet retain their positions, flat upon the ground, the right leg is straightened, the left knee bent, and the body advanced over the left knee as far as possible consistent with stability. The left shoulder is necessarily somewhat in advance of the right, and the arms are stretched out horizontally, and quite on a level with the shoulders. The barrel of the rifle, too, is to be held horizontally, with the bayonet pointing to the adversary's throat and chest.

In Fig. 36 we have the point from guard with the lunge, which ought to give an extra reach of a foot or more. Here, as in the point without the lunge, the sole of the right foot should remain flat upon the ground, whilst the left is advanced about a foot or fifteen inches smartly on the straight line between the right heel and the adversary.

FIG. 36.—POINT, WITH LUNGE

It is most important to remember that in all lunges the step-out should be bold and decided, but that to over-stretch the distance is worse than stepping short, because it leaves one in a position from which it is hard to recover. Having made your attack, you want to be in a position of easy retreat to the base of operations, which is "on guard."

We next come to what is called the "Throw-point," by which a little extra reach is obtained over the ordinary point with lunge. This is a point which may be very effective, but unless a man is strong in the arm he should not use it much on account of the difficulty in rapidly regaining hold of the rifle with both hands. The throw-point comes in when in making the ordinary lunge you feel that you are going to be just ever so little short; you then release

FIG. 37.—THROW POINT

FIG. 38.—GUARD—OPPOSED TO SWORDSMAN

your hold of the barrel with the left hand, and, bringing the right shoulder well forward, you continue the lunge, holding the rifle by the thin part of the stock alone. The *very instant* your right arm is *fully* extended, and the point of the bayonet has reached its furthest limit, you should draw back the rifle, regain possession of the barrel with the left hand, and come into the "on guard" position.

As previously hinted, a knowledge of fencing is of the first importance in studying the use of weapons where the point is the main factor, and the longer the weapon the more this fact is forced upon us. It is of course true for all weapons, but the leverage being so great in the case of the rifle and bayonet, it becomes more apparent. For example, the slightest touch from the thin blade of a foil is sufficient, when applied near the point of the bayonet, to bring about the necessary deflection of the weapon. Indeed I cannot help thinking that if two men fought, one armed with the small-sword or light rapier and the other with the rifle and bayonet, the swordsman would win—always supposing that they were equally expert in the use of their respective weapons. It would seem that the lightness and consequent "handiness" of the rapier must more than make up for the length and strength of the more ponderous arm.

FIG. 39.—SHORTEN ARMS

Conflicts between the sword and bayonet are common enough, but it is the broad-sword, as a rule; and one does not often see the bayonet, opposed to the small-sword, used exclusively for thrusting.

In Fig. 38 is given the best general position for coming on guard when opposed by a swordsman. The great object is to keep the opponent at a distance; directly he gets *your* side of your point you are in difficulties. Therefore never let the point of your bayonet wander far from the lines leading straight to his body.

There is, of course, the "Shorten-arms," shown in Fig. 39; but in actual conflict you might be a dead man twice over before you could get the bayonet back to the position indicated. When the

FIG. 40.—LOW GUARD

FIG. 41.—POINT FROM LOW GUARD

swordsman gets to close quarters, and has possibly missed you, a
good plan is to knock him down with the butt of the rifle—using
the weapon like the quarter-staff (*vide* Fig. 9).

The next two sketches show the positions in "Low Guard" and
"Point from Low Guard"—the latter being particularly effective
on broken ground when an enemy is rushing up a hill at you, or
when you want to spike a fellow hiding in long grass.

The "High Guard" and "Head Parry" are chiefly used when
dealing with cavalry. It seems to me hardly necessary to give the

FIG. 42.—HIGH GUARD—
OPPOSED TO MOUNTED MAN

FIG. 43.—HEAD PARRY

points of these guards, as they simply amount to extending the arms straight in the direction of the foe.

A man on foot possesses one or two great advantages over a mounted man, for his movements are quicker, and if he can only avoid being ridden down and can keep on the horseman's bridle-hand side, he ought to have a good chance of delivering his point in the left side. It is most important that the man on foot should be ready to spring back so as to avoid a sudden sweep to the left, which will bring him, if the horse is spurred forward at the same time, right under the rider's sword arm.

It is almost superfluous to add that in practice the general habiliments should be much the same as those used when playing quarter-staff. In the illustrations the hands are left bare in order to show the grip of the rifle, but boxing-gloves should invariably be worn, or a broken finger may be the result.

CHAPTER 6

The Cudgel

One remembers reading somewhere, I think in Bunyan's *Pilgrim's Progress*, of a certain "grievous crab-tree cudgel," and the impression left by this description is that the weapon, gnarled and knotty, was capable of inflicting grievous bodily harm.

Any thick stick under two feet long, such as a watchman's staff or a policeman's truncheon, may be fairly called a cudgel, and it is not so long ago that cudgel-play formed one of the chief attractions at country fairs in many parts of England.

A stage was erected, and the young fellows of the neighbourhood were wont to try conclusions with their friends or those celebrities from more distant parts of the country who were anxious to lower their colours.

The game was at times pretty rough, and the object of each combatant was to break the skin on the scalp or forehead of his antagonist, *so as to cause blood to flow.* As soon as the little red stream was seen to trickle down the face of one or other the battle was at an end, and the man who was successful in drawing first blood was declared the victor. Similarly, German students, squabbling over love affairs or other trivial matters, fight with a long sort of foil, which has a very short lancet blade at the extreme point. Their object, like our old cudgel-players, is to draw first blood, only our Teutonic cousins, in drawing the blood, often lop off their friends' noses or slit open their cheeks from ear to mouth.

There is a great similarity in these two games, because in each the head, and the head alone, is the object aimed at. In the one case the defeated party went away with a pretty severe bump on his head, and in the other he hies him to a surgeon to have his nose fixed on, or his cheek stitched up with silver wire.

I have never been fortunate enough to witness a bout with the cudgels, but those who have been more lucky say that the combatants stood very close to each other, making all the hits nearly straight on to the top of their adversaries' heads, and guarding the returns and attacks with their cudgels and with their left arms.

Considering the cudgel as a modern weapon, I am inclined to advocate its use for prodding an enemy in the pit of the stomach, for, with the extra eighteen inches or so of reach which your cudgel gives you, it is likely that you may get your thrust well home, at any rate before the opponent can hit you with his fist. Many of us know what a blow on the "mark" with the naked fist will do. Well, the area of the knuckles is very much greater than the area of the end of even a very stout stick, so that, if you can put anything like the same force into the thrust that you can into the blow, you will bring a smaller area to bear on a vital point, and consequently work on that point with greater effect.

A grievous crab-tree (or blackthorn) cudgel, with two or three ounces of lead let into one end, is a good thing to have under your pillow at night. Armed with this instrument, you can steal up behind your burglar whilst he is opening your wife's jewel case or bagging your favourite gold snuff-box; but don't get excited about it, and remember to hit his head rather on the *sides* than on the back or front.

Some authorities advocate "life-preservers," but later on I hope to give my reasons for not caring much about this combination of lead and cane.

THE SHILLELAGH

In Ireland they were formerly very partial to the use of the *shillelagh*, and even to this day there is a little bit of fun in this line to be seen at most of the fairs.

The *shillelagh* proper is about four feet long and is usually made of blackthorn, oak, ash, or hazel; and it is a great point to get it uniform in thickness and in weight throughout its entire length. It is held somewhere about eight inches or so from the centre, and my countrymen, who are always pretty active on their pins when fighting, use their left forearms to protect the left side of their heads.

It is extraordinary what a lot of knocking about a sturdy Irishman can put up with, and what whacks he can receive on the head without any apparent damage. One cannot help thinking that the Celtic skull must be thicker than the Saxon. The brains in the former are certainly more capable than those in the latter of producing brilliant and amusing, if incorrect, ideas and expressions. The history of the Emerald Isle swarms with Boyle-Rocheisms as the country itself has long been said to swarm with absentee landlords.

After a certain fair, where the whisky and the whacks had contended pretty severely for the first place as regards strength, a certain Paddy was found lying, as Mrs. Malaprop would say, "in a state of como," in a ditch hard by the scene of conflict. A friend solicitous, and fearing the worst, said, "Och, Paddy, what ails ye? Are ye dead?" A feeble voice replied, "Ochone, no, Jack. I'm not dead, but I'm spacheless."

The length of the *shillelagh* gives it a great advantage over a shorter stick, for, when held about a third of its length from the end, the shorter portion serves to guard the right side of the head and the right forearm. Indeed, the definition of the quarter-staff, given at the commencement of chapter 2., seems to me to apply far better to the *shillelagh*, which may in a sense be regarded as the link between the ordinary walking-stick and the mighty weapon which Robin Hood wielded so deftly in his combat with Little John.

The use of the point is almost unknown in Irish conflicts. My countrymen twirl their *shillelaghs* above their heads with a whirring noise, and endeavour to knock off their opponents' hats so as to get at their heads. Then begins the fun of the fair—all is slashing and whacking, and the hardest skull generally comes off the best. Sometimes a great deal of skill is displayed, and I often wonder whether a really expert swordsman would be much more than a match for some quick, strong, Kerry boys I could pick out. Be it remembered, a swordsman invariably keeps his left hand behind his back, whilst an Irishman nearly always makes his left forearm the guard for the left side of his head, and so has more scope for hitting than he would otherwise have. One is here reminded of the conflict between Fitz-James and the Highland Chieftain, Roderick Dhu:

> *Ill fared it then with Roderick Dhu,*
> *That on the field his targe he threw,*
> *Whose brazen studs and tough bull-hide*
> *Had death so often dashed aside;*
> *For, trained abroad his arms to wield,*
> *Fitz-James's blade was sword and shield.*

The left arm, supplying the place of the *targe*, alluded to in Scott's lines, is doubtless an advantage; but, in the case of the two combatants whose merits we are considering, the ordinary swordsman possesses superior reach, can lunge out further, and knows full well the value of the point.

THE FUN OF THE FAIR—"WHIRROO."

A melee at an Irish fair is worth seeing, but it is better not to join in it, if possible.

A number of the "boys," from Cork or an adjacent county, were once had up before Judge Keogh for beating a certain man within an inch of his life. A witness under examination—after graphically describing how one of the prisoners had beaten the poor man "wid a stone, and he lying senseless in the road;" how another had hit the "crater wid a thick wattle;" and how a third had kicked him in the back—was asked what one Michael O'Flannagan, another of the prisoners, had done. "Begorra, your honour," said the witness, "devil a hap'orth was Micky doing at all, at all; he was just walking round searching for a vacancy."

A similar story is told of about a dozen tinkers who had set upon one man and were unmercifully beating him. Presently there was a lull in the proceedings, and a little deformed man, brandishing a very big stick, elbowed his way through the crowd, shouting, "Och, now, boys, for the love of mercy let a poor little cripple have just one stroke at him."

THE WALKING-STICK

The choice of this useful adjunct is by no means as easy as many people suppose, for it involves not only a knowledge of the prerequisites—in the matter of various kinds of woods, etc.—but also an acquaintance with the situations a man may find himself in, and the uses to which he may have to put his walking-stick.

First, then, as to the matter of the best wood. There are, roughly speaking, two headings under which we may class our types of raw material—strong and stiff wood, such as the oak and the hazel; and strong and pliable, such as the ash-plant and various kinds of canes. What one really wants to secure is a sufficient amount of stiffness and strength to enable one to make an effective hit or *longe*, without any chance of snapping, and a degree of pliability and spring combined with that lightness which makes a stick handy and lively in actual encounter.

The oak has plenty of power and about the right density, but, unless you get a rather big stick—too big for all-round usefulness,—it is apt to snap. The hazel is perhaps rather too stiff, and it is certainly too light, though for this very reason it is *handy*. Then, again, there is no bending a hazel without a great chance of breaking it. A good strong ground-ash is not to be despised if cut at the right time, but it is always apt to split or break. Turning to the rattan-cane, we find a capital solid cane—almost unbreakable—but with rather *too* much bend in it for thrusting, or warding off the rush of a savage dog. The rattan, too, is very apt to split if by any chance the ferrule comes off; and when once it has *really* split you might just as well have a birch-rod in your hands.

Where, then, shall we look for a stick which combines all the good qualities and is free from the drawbacks just enumerated? Without the slightest hesitation I refer you to the Irish blackthorn, which can be chosen of such convenient size and weight as not to be cumbersome, and which, if carefully selected, possesses all the strength of the oak, plus enormous toughness, and a pliability which makes it a truly charming weapon to work with.

It is a matter of some difficulty to obtain a *real* blackthorn in London or any big town. You go into a shop, and they show you a smart-looking stick which has been peeled and deprived of most of its knobs, dyed black, and varnished. That is *not* the genuine article, and, if you buy it, you will become the possessor of a stick as inferior to a blackthorn as a pewter skewer is inferior to a Damascus blade.

The best way is to send over to Kerry, Cork, or some other county in the Emerald Isle, and ask a friend to secure the proper thing as *prepared by the inhabitants*.

The sticks are cut out of the hedges at that time of year when the sap is not rising; they are then carefully prepared and dried in the peat smoke for some considerable time, the bark of course being left on and the knobs not cut off too close; and, when ready, they are hard, tough, and thoroughly reliable weapons.

As regards appearance, too, I think, when the hard surface of the rich-coloured bark has been rubbed up with a little oil and a nice silver mount fixed on the handle, no man need feel ashamed of being seen with one of them in Piccadilly or Bond Street.

The section of these sticks is seldom a true circle, but bear in mind, when giving your order, to ask for those which are *rather flat than otherwise*. I mean that the section should be elliptical, and not circular. The shape of the stick then more nearly approaches that of the blade of a sabre, and if you understand sword exercise and make all cuts and guards with the true edge, you are far more likely to do effective work.

Again, the blow comes in with greater severity on account of the curvature at either end of the major axis of the ellipse being sharper than it is at the end of any diameter of the circle, the sectional areas, of course, being taken as equal.

The length of the blackthorn depends on the length of the man for whom it is intended, but always go in for a good long stick. Useful lengths range between 2 ft. 10 in. and 3 ft., and even 3 ft. 6 in. for a very tall man.

The blackthorn, being stiff and covered with sharp knots, is a first-rate weapon for defence at very close quarters. When, therefore, your efforts at distance-work have failed, and you begin to be "hemmed in," seize the stick very firmly with both hands, and dash the point and hilt alternately into the faces and sides of your opponents.

Always have a good ferrule at the end of your stick. An inch and a half from an old gun barrel is the best; and do not fix it on by means of a rivet running through the stick. Let it be fixed in its place either by a deep dent in the side, or by cutting out two little notches and pressing the saw-like tooth into the wood. It is also a good plan to carry these saw-like teeth all round the ferrule and then press the points well into the wood; there is then no chance of the fastening-on causing a split or crack in the wood.

The weight of the stick is an important matter to consider. Some blackthorns are so enormously heavy that it is next to impossible to do any quick effective work with them, and one is reminded, on seeing a man "over sticked,"—if I may be allowed such an expression—of Lord Dundreary's riddle, "Why does a dog wag his tail? Because the dog is stronger than the tail," or of David in Saul's armour. Some time ago it was rather the fashion for very young men to affect gigantic walking-sticks—possibly with the view of intimidating would-be plunderers and robbers, and investing themselves generally with a magic sort of *noli me tangere* air.

Without wishing to detract from the undoubted merits, *in certain special cases*, of these very big sticks, I am bound to say that, only being useful to a limited extent, they should not be encouraged. Let the stick you habitually carry be one well within your compass. If it comes up to guard readily and without any apparent effort or straining of your wrist, and if you find you can make all the broadsword cuts, grasping it as shown in Fig. 14, without the least spraining your thumb, then you may be pretty sure that you are not "over-sticked," and that your cuts and thrusts will be smart to an extent not to be acquired if you carried a stick ever so little too heavy for you.

Though it is a good plan to be accustomed to the feel of the weapon which is most likely to serve you in time of need, it is nevertheless a grand mistake to get into a way of imagining that you can only use one kind of stick or one kind of sword effectively.

This is one reason why it is so advisable to range wide in fencing matters. I would always say, commence with the foils and work hard, under some good master, for a year or so without touching any other branch. Then go on to broad-sword, and keep to alternate days with foils. Later on take up the single-stick, and then go on to bayonet-exercise, quarter-staff, and anything else you please.

This extended range of work will give you a wonderful general capability for adapting yourself at a moment's notice to any weapon chance may place in your hands: the leg of an old chair, the joint of a fishing rod, or the common or garden spade; any of these may be used with great effect by an accomplished all-round swordsman.

There is one point on which a few words may not be out of place in this connection.

Good men, with their fists, and those who are proficient with the sword or stick, often complain that, in actual conflict with the rough and ready, though ignorant, assailant, they are worsted because the adversary does something diametrically opposed to what a scientific exponent of either art would do in similar circumstances.

It is certainly trying, when you square up to a rough and expect him to hit out with his fists, to receive a violent doubling-up kick in the stomach; and similarly annoying is it, when attacked by a man with a stick, to experience treatment quite different to anything you ever came across in your own particular School-of-Arms.

But after all this is only what you ought to expect. It is absolutely necessary to suit yourself to your environment for the time being, and be ready for *anything*.

Depend upon it science must tell, and there is always this very consoling reflection to fall back upon: if your opponent misses you, or you are quick enough to avoid his clumsy attack—either of which is extremely likely to happen—it is highly probable that you will be able to make good your own attack, for, as a rule, the unscientific man hits out of distance or wide of the mark, and this is rarely the case with a scientific man.

It once fell to my lot to be set upon by a couple of very disagreeable roughs in Dublin, one of whom did manage to get the first blow, but it was "all round" and did not do much harm. Before he could deliver a second hit I managed to lay him out with a very severe cut from my blackthorn, which came in contact with his head just between the rim of his hat and the collar of his coat. Now, had my knowledge of stick-play been insufficient to enable me to accurately direct this cut (cut 5) to its destination, I might not now be scribbling these pages. As it turned out, this poor injured rough was placed *hors de combat*, and was afterwards conveyed to the hospital, and I only had to tackle his friend, a stubborn varlet, who, after knocking me about a good deal and also receiving some rough treatment at my hands, ran away. He was "wanted" by the police for some time, but was never caught.

This little episode is only given to show that the proper delivery of one blow or hit is often enough to turn the tables, and how advisable it is to practise *often*, so as to keep the eye and hand both steady and quick.

When walking along a country road it is a good plan to make cuts with your stick at weeds, etc., in the hedges, always using the true edge, *i.e.* if aiming at a certain part of a bramble or nettle, to cut at it, just as though you were using a sabre. By this sort of practice, which, by the way, is to be deprecated in a young plantation or in a friend's garden, you may greatly increase the accuracy of your eye.

It is merely an application of the principle which enables a fly-fisher to place his fly directly under such and such over-hanging boughs, or gives the experienced driver such control over his whip that he can flick a midge off the ear of one of his galloping leaders.

Much does not, in all probability, depend upon the success or failure of the *piscator's* cast, and very likely the midge might safely be allowed to remain on the leader's ear; but if you are walking in a lonely suburb or country lane, your *life* may depend upon the accuracy with which you can deliver one single cut or thrust with your faithful blackthorn.

I can almost hear people say, "Oh, this is all rubbish; I'm not going to be attacked; life would not be worth living if one had to be always 'on guard' in this way." Well, considering that this world, from the time we are born to the time we die, is made up of uncertainties, and that we are never really secure from attack at any moment of our lives, it does seem worth while to devote a little attention to the pursuit of a science, which is not only healthful and most fascinating, but which may, in a second of time, enable you to turn a defeat into a victory, and save yourself from being mauled and possibly killed in a fight which was none of your own making. Added to all this, science gives a consciousness of power and ability to assist the weak and defenceless, which ought to be most welcome to the mind of any man. Though always anxious to avoid anything like "a row," there are times when it may be necessary to interfere for the sake of humanity, and how much more easy is it to make that interference dignified and effective if you take your stand with a certainty that you can, if pushed to extreme measures, make matters very warm indeed for the aggressor? The consciousness of power gives you your real authority, and with it you are far more likely to be calm and to gain your point than you would be without the knowledge. Backed up by science, you can both talk and act in a way which is likely to lead to a peaceful solution of a difficulty, whereas, if the science is absent, you *dare* not, from very uncertainty, use those very words which you know ought to be used on the occasion.

There are necessarily a good many difficulties to be faced in becoming at all proficient in the art of self-defence, but the advantages to be gained are doubtless very great.

An expert swordsman, and by this I mean one who is really *au fait* with any weapon you may put into his hand, who is also a good boxer and wrestler, is a very nasty customer for any one or even two footpads to make up to.

The worst of it is that it takes so long to become really good in any branch of athletics. When you know all, or nearly all, that is to be learned, you get a bit stiff and past work! But this, after all, need not trouble one much, since it applies to all relations of life. As a wise man once said, with a touch of sorrow and regret in his tone, "By the time you have learned how to live, you die."

THE UMBRELLA

As a weapon of modern warfare this implement has not been given a fair place. It has, indeed, too often been spoken of with contempt and disdain, but there is no doubt that, even in the hands of a strong and angry old woman, a gamp of solid proportions may be the cause of much damage to an adversary. Has not an umbrella, opened suddenly and with a good flourish, stopped the deadly onslaught of the infuriated bull, and caused the monarch of the fields to turn tail? Has it not, when similarly brought into action, been the means of stopping a runaway horse, whose mad career might otherwise have caused many broken legs and arms?

If, then, there are these uses beyond those which the dampness of our insular climate forces upon us, it may be well to inquire how they can be brought to bear when a man, who is an expert swordsman, or one who has given attention to his fencing lessons, is attacked without anything in his hands save the homely umbrella.

It is, of course, an extremely risky operation prodding a fellow-creature in the eye with the point of an umbrella; and I once knew a man who, being attacked by many roughs, and in danger of losing his life through their brutality, in a despairing effort made a desperate thrust at the face of one of his assailants. The point entered the eye *and the brain*, and the man fell stone dead at his feet. I would therefore only advocate the thrusting when extreme danger threatens—as a *dernier resort*, in fact, and when it is a case of who shall be killed, you or your assailant.

There are two methods of using the umbrella, *viz.* holding it like a fencing foil—and for this reason umbrellas should always be chosen with strong straight handles—for long thrusts when at a distance, or grasping it firmly with both hands, as one grasps the military rifle when at bayonet-exercise. In the latter case one has a splendid weapon for use against several assailants at close quarters. Both the arms should be bent and held close to the body, which should be made to work freely from the hips, so as to put plenty of weight into the short sharp prods with which you can alternately visit your opponents' faces and ribs. If you have the handle in your right hand, and the left hand grasps the silk (or alpaca), not more than a foot from the point, it will be found most effective to use the forward and upward strokes with the point for the faces, and the back-thrusts with the handle for the bodies. Whatever you do, let your strokes be made very quickly and forcibly, for when it comes to such close work as this your danger lies in being altogether overpowered, thrown down, and possibly kicked to death; and, as I have before hinted, when there is a choice of evils, choose the lesser, and don't be the least squeamish about hurting those who will not hesitate to make a football of your devoted head should it unfortunately be laid low.

Then, again, there is no better weapon for guarding a heavy blow aimed at you with a thick bludgeon than an umbrella, which, with its wire ribs and soft covering, is almost unbreakable, when all its ribs are held tightly with *both* hands; it is also, for the same reason, when thus grasped with both hands, an excellent defence against the attack of a large powerful dog, which may spring at your throat; but, in this case, remember to get one of your legs well behind the other so as to bring most of the weight of your body on the foremost leg, and, if you are lucky, you may have the satisfaction of throwing the animal on his back.

Thrusting, prodding, and guarding, then, may be called the strong points of the gamp; it is no use for hitting purposes, and invariably tumbles to pieces, comes undone, and gets into a demoralized condition when one tries to make it fulfil all the conditions of the unclothed walking-stick. Besides which, the handles are *never* made strong enough for hitting, and the hittee is protected by the folds of silk.

Hitting, then, is the weak point of the gamp. Try to remember this when you feel inclined to administer a castigation to man or beast, and bear in mind that a comic scene may ensue, when, hot and angry, you stand with your best umbrella broken and half open, with the silk torn and the ribs sticking out in all directions.

Sometimes umbrellas have been made even more effective weapons by what is called a spring dagger, which consists of a short, strong knife or dirk let into the handle, and is readily brought into play by a sudden jerk, or by touching a spring. This may be all very well for travellers in the out-of-the-way regions of Spain, Sicily, or Italy, but I don't like these dangerous accessories for English use, as they *may* be unfortunately liable to abuse by excitable persons.

In addition to the weapons already alluded to, there are others which, though not so generally known, or so generally useful, may be turned to good account on certain occasions.

The "life-preserver" consists of a stout piece of cane about a foot long, with a ball of five or six ounces of lead attached firmly to one end by catgut netting, whilst the other end is furnished with a strong leather or catgut loop to go round the wrist and prevent the weapon flying from or being snatched from the hand.

Of course this instrument *may* be very effective, very deadly, but what you have to consider is this: the serviceable portion is so small—no bigger than a hen's egg—that unless you are almost an expert, or circumstances greatly favour you, there is more than a chance of altogether missing your mark. With the life-preserver you have, say, at most a couple of inches only of effective weapon to rely on, whereas with the cudgel at least a foot of hard and heavy wood may be depended upon for bowling over the adversary.

A leaded rattan cane is a dangerous instrument in expert hands, but my objections to it are very similar to those advanced with regard to the shorter weapon. Leaded walking-sticks are not "handy," for the presence of so much weight in the hitting portion makes them extremely bad for quick returns, recovery, and for guarding purposes.

To my mind the leaded rattan is to the well-chosen blackthorn what the life-preserver is to the cudgel—an inferior weapon.

One does not want to *kill* but to *disable*, even those who have taken the mean advantage of trying to catch one unprepared in the highways and byways. To take an ordinary common-sense view of the matter: it is surely better far to have a three to one chance in favour of disabling than an even chance of killing a fellow-creature? The disablement is all you want, and, having secured that, the best thing is to get out of the way as soon as possible, so as to avoid further complications.

The sword-stick is an instrument I thoroughly detest and abominate, and could not possibly advocate the use of in any circumstances whatever.

These wretched apologies for swords are to outward appearance ordinary straight canes—usually of Malacca cane. On pulling the handle of one of these weapons, however, a nasty piece of steel is revealed, and then you draw forth a blade something between a fencing-foil and a skewer.

They are poor things as regards length and strength, and "not in it" with a good solid stick. In the hands of a hasty, hot-tempered individual they may lead to the shedding of blood over some trivial, senseless squabble. The hollowing out of the cane, to make the scabbard, renders them almost useless for hitting purposes.

In the environs of our big cities there is always a chance of attack by some fellow who asks the time, wants a match to light his cigar, or asks the way to some place. When accosted never stop, never draw out watch or box of lights, and never know the way anywhere. Always make a good guess at the time, and swear you have no matches about you. It is wonderful to notice kind-hearted ladies stopping to give to stalwart beggars who are only waiting for an opportunity to snatch purses, and it would be interesting to know how many annually lose their purses and watches through this mistaken method of distributing largess.

Let me conclude by saying that, if you want to be as safe as possible in a doubtful neighbourhood, your best friends are a quick ear, a quick eye, a quick step, and a predilection for the middle of the road. The two former help you to detect, as the two latter may enable you to avoid a sudden onslaught. In et aliquate feui tat lummodo ecte magna acil ex ea conse dit lor incilit am quat volorperat adion velit nonulputem vel ercip esenibh ex elit lutet alit ad ea autpatum qui tat. Ut ilit lore modolut atumsandrem inim dignissis adip er sit wisim quis nos nons am aliquamet vulputa tueriustis nos nulla con henit wisci te vullupt atincin ulputpat wisi er inibh eraesequi bla faciduipit nullaore eros ad ming et prat. Ut euis esed mod min henissit veliquat.

Equisissed dionsecte consequat dolorti onsequis ad tat, quam, sequis nullaor irit ute eu feugait ing ex el dions euguero commod ercilisci ent adit duismod tem quate tatincilisi euisl er sequi ent iril in hent nos alit vulla con ea faccum qui erate dolore volore delendigna consequat. Duisisis nismodolor aut wisi eliquam ing ecte magna feugiam illamet volore ming ex ea ad moloborem velit

The Art of Fencing

Monsieur L'Abbat

Preface

I thought it very suitable to my business, when I met with so good an author as Monsieur L'Abbat, on the art of fencing, to publish his rules, which in general, will I believe be very useful, not only as they may contribute to the satisfaction of such gentlemen as are already proficients in the art, and to the better discipline of those who intend to become so, but also in regard that the nicety and exactness of his rules, for the most part, and their great consistency with reason, may, and will in all probability, lay a regular and good foundation for future masters, who though accustomed to any particular method formerly practised, may rather choose to proceed upon the authority of an excellent master, than upon a vain and mistaken confidence of their own perfection, or upon an obstinate refusal to submit to rules founded on, and demonstrated by reason.

For my part, though I had my instructions from the late Mr. Hillary Tully of London, who was (and I think with great reason) esteemed a most eminent master in his time, I thought I could not make too nice a scrutiny into my profession, by comparing notes with Monsieur L'Abbat, which improved me in some points, and confirmed me and others, to my no small satisfaction, being well persuaded, that, as a professor of this science, it would have been an unpardonable fault in me to deprive our nations of such an improvement, either through prejudice to his, or partiality to my own opinion.

Though I have already said that Mr. L'Abbat's rules are nice, reasonable, and demonstrative, yet I would not have it inferred from thence, that he approves of them all, as really essential to the art of fencing; there being some which he does not approve of, and which he would not have mentioned, had they not interfered with his profession, by the practice and recommendation of some masters, who being more capricious than knowing, were fonder of the showy or superficial, than of the solid part of the science.

Volting, passing, and lowering the body, are three things which Mr. L'Abbat disapproves of, in which opinion I join; because the sword being the instrument of defence, there can be no safety when the proper opposition of the blade is wanting, as it is in *volting* and lowering the body, and in passing, by reason of the weakness of the situation, which cannot produce a vigorous action.

Notwithstanding which, there is a modern master, who as soon as he had seen this book, and the attitudes representing *volting*, passing and lowering the body, began and still continues teaching them to his scholars, without considering how unsafe and dangerous they are, for want of the proper opposition of the sword when within measure.

Of all professions, that of arms has in all ages, since their invention, been esteemed the noblest and most necessary; it being by them that the laws preserve their force, that our dominions are defended from the encroachments of our enemies, and ill designing people kept in the subjection due to their sovereigns; and of all arms, the sword is probably the most ancient: it is honourable and useful, and upon occasion, causes a greater acquisition of glory than any other: it is likewise worn by kings and princes, as an ornament to majesty and grandeur, and a mark of their courage, and distinguishes the nobility from the lower rank of men.

It is the most useful, having the advantage of fire arms, in that it is as well defensive as offensive, whereas they carry no defence with them; and it is far preferable to pikes and other long weapons, not only because it is more weildy and easy of carriage, but also by reason of the perfection to which art has brought the use of the small sword; there being no exercise that conduces so much as fencing, to strengthen and supple the parts, and to give the body an easy and graceful appearance.

The Sword, since it's first invention, has been used in different manners: first, with a shield or buckler; secondly, with a helmet, and thirdly, with a dagger, which is still used in Spain and Italy. Mr. Patinotris, who taught at Rome, introduced, and laid down rules for the use of the small sword alone, which has since been much improved by the French and our nations.

As the art of fencing consists in attacking and defending with the sword, it is necessary that every motion and situation tend to these two principal points, *viz.* In offending to be defended, and in defending to be in an immediate condition to offend.

There is no guard but has it's thrust, and no thrust without it's parade, no parade without it's feint, no feint without it's opposite time or motion, no opposite time or motion but has it's counter, and there is even a counter to that counter.

Some injudicious persons have objected to Mr. L'Abbat's manner of fencing, that it is too beautiful and nice, without observing that if it be beautiful, it cannot be dangerous, beauty consisting in rule, and rule in the safety of attacking and defending.

In fencing, there are five figures of the wrist, *viz. prime, seconde, tierce, quart,* and *quinte.* The first is of very little use, and the last of none at all. *Prime* is the figure that the wrist is in, in drawing the Sword. *seconde* and *tierce* require one and the same figure of the wrist, with this difference only, that in *seconde,* the wrist must be raised higher, in order to oppose the adversary's sword; but in both these thrusts the thumb nail must be turned directly down, and the edges of the blade of the foil of an equal height.

Quart is the handsomest figure in fencing, the thumb nail and the flat of the foil being directly up, and the wrist supported so as to cover the body below as well as above. In *quinte,* the Wrist is more turned and raised that in *quart,* which uncovers the body, and weakens the point, and therefore is not used by the skilful.

Some masters divide the blade into three parts, *viz.* the *fort,* the *feeble,* and the middle. Others divide it into four, *viz.* the *fort,* the half *fort,* the *feeble,* and the half *feeble;* but to avoid perplexity, I divide it only into *fort* and *feeble;* though it may be divided into as many parts as there are degrees of *fort* and *feeble* to be found on the blade.

The attitudes which are in the book, are copied exactly from the originals; though I might perhaps have made some alterations, in my opinion, for the better, yet I chose rather to leave them as they are, than to run the hazard of spoiling any of them: I have therefore left the same bend in the foils as Mr. L'Abbat recommends, *and for which he makes an apology in his preface.*

Nor have I, in any of the attitudes, represented a left-handed figure, because by looking through the paper on the blank side, they will appear reversed, and consequently left-handed.

Monsieur L'Abbat recommends the turning on the edge of the left-foot in a lunge, as may be seen by the attitudes. This method indeed was formerly practised by all masters, and would be very good, if their scholars had not naturally run into an error, by turning the foot so much as to bring the ankle to the ground, whereby the foot became so weak as to make the recovery difficult, for want of a sufficient support from the left-foot, which, in recovering, bears the whole weight of the body: therefore I would not advise the turning on the edge of the foot to any but such as, by long practice on the flat, are able to judge of the strength of their situation, and consequently, will not turn the foot more than is consistent therewith.

It may sometimes be necessary to turn on the edge, on such ground whereon the flat would slip, and the edge would not, if it were properly turned; but even in this case, by turning it too much it would have no hold of the terrace, and therefore would be as dangerous as keeping it on the flat.

The chief reason for turning on the edge, is that the length of the lunge is greater by about three inches, which a man who is a judge of measure need never have recourse to, because he will not push but when he knows he is within reach.

Some of the subscribing gentlemen will, perhaps, be surprised, when they find this book published in my name, after having taken receipts, for the first moiety of their subscription money, in the name of Mr. Campbell, to whom I am obliged for his assistance in the translation, he being a better master of the French tongue than I am. Indeed to the chief reasons why they were not signed in my name, are, first, because I was, at the time of their being signed, a stranger in this city, being then lately come from England. And secondly, lest I should meet with such opposition as might perhaps have frustrated my design of publishing this book, I thought proper to conceal my being concerned in it, until Mr. Campbell had shown the translation to all the principal masters in town, and gained their approbation much in favour of it.

CHAPTER 1
Of Choosing and Mounting a Blade

Courage and skill being often of little use without a good weapon, I think it necessary, before I lay down rules for using it, to show how to choose a good blade, and how it ought to be mounted.

The length of the blade ought to be proportionable to the stature of the person who is to use it: the longest sword, from point to pommel, should reach perpendicularly from the ground to the navel, and the shortest, to the waist; being large in proportion to its length, and not extremely large, nor very small, as some people wear them; the over large blades being unwieldy, unless very hollow, which makes them weak, and the narrow ones being not sufficient to cover the body enough.

In order to choose a good blade, three things are to be observed: first, that the blade have no flaw in it, especially across, it being more dangerous so than length-way.

Secondly, that it be well tempered, which you'll know by bending it against a wall or other place; if it bend only towards the point, it is faulty, but if it bend in a semicircular manner, and the blade spring back to its straightness, it is a good sign; if it remains bent it is a fault, though not so great as if it did not bend at all; for a blade that bends being of a soft temper, seldom breaks; but a stiff one being hard tempered is easily broke.

The third observation is to be made by breaking the point, and if the part broken be of a grey colour, the steel is good; if it be white it is not: or you may strike the blade with a key or other piece of iron, and if he gives a clear sound, there is no hidden fault in it. In bending a blade you must not force it, what I have said being sufficient to know it by, and besides by forcing it, it may be so weakened in some part as to break when it comes to be used.

it would not be amiss for a man to see his sword mounted, because the cutlers, to save themselves the trouble of filing the inside of the hilts and pommel, to make the holes wider, often file the tongue[1] of the blade too much, and fill up the vacancies with bits of wood, by which means the sword is not firm in the hand, and the tongue being thin and weak, is apt to break in parrying or on a dry beat, as has been unhappily experienced. Care should also be taken that the end of the tongue be well riveted to the extremity of the pommel, lest the grip should fly off, which would be of very dangerous consequence.

Some men choose straight blades, others will have them bending a little upwards or downwards; some like them to bend a little in the *fort*, and others in the *feeble*, which is commonly called *le Tour de Breteur*, or the Bullie's blade. The shell should be proportionable in bigness to the blade, and of a metal that will resist a point, and the handle fitted to the hand.

Some like square handles, and others choose round ones; the square are better and firmer in the hand, but as this difference depends on fancy, as does also the bow, which in some cases may preserve the hand, but may be a hindrance in inclosing, I shall leave it to the decision of the fashions.

---

1. The iron at the end of the blade that runs into the handle.

CHAPTER 2
Of Guard

By guard, is meant such a situation of all the parts of the body as enables them to give their mutual assistance to defend or attack. A guard cannot be perfect without a good and graceful disposition, proceeding from a natural proportion of the parts of the body, and an easy and vigorous motion, which is to be acquired by practice, and the instruction of a good master.

As In all bodily exercises, a good air, freedom, vigour, and a just disposition of the body and limbs are necessary, so are they more especially in fencing, the least disorder in this case being of the worst consequence; and the guard being the centre whence all the vigour should proceed, and which should communicate strength and agility to every part of the body, if there be the least irregularity in any one part, there cannot be that agreeableness, power of defence, justness, or swiftness that is requisite.

In order to be well in guard, it is absolutely necessary that the feet, as the foundation that conduces chiefly to communicate freedom and strength to the other parts, be placed at such a distance from each other, and in such a lineal manner as may be advantageous: the distance must be about two foot from one heel to the other; for if it were greater, the adversary, though of the same stature, and with a sword of equal length, would be within measure when you would not, which would be a very considerable fault, measure being one of the principal parts of fencing, and if the feet were nearer together, you would want strength, which is also a great fault, because a *feeble* situation cannot produce a vigorous action.

The line must be taken from the hindmost part of the right heel

PLATE 1
TOP: THE MIDDLING GUARD
BOTTOM: THE STRAIGHT GUARD OR FLAT SWORD

to the left heel near the ankle, the point of the right foot must be opposite to the adversary's, turning out the point of the left foot, and bending the left knee over the point of the same foot, keeping the right knee a little bent, that it may have a freedom of motion.

The body must be upright, which gives it a better air, greater strength, and more liberty to advance and retire, being supported almost equally by the two feet. Some masters teach to keep the body back in favour of measure, which cannot be broke by the body when it is already drawn back, though it is often necessary, not only to avoid a surprise, but also to deceive a man of superior swiftness who pushes a just length: therefore it is much better to have the liberty of retiring to avoid the thrusts of the adversary, or of extricating yourself by advancing towards him and pushing (as I shall observe in its proper place) than to keep the body in one situation at a distance, which being fixed, cannot deceive a person who knows any thing of measure; moreover, such a retention of the body does not only hinder the breaking measure with the body, but also the left leg is so oppressed with its whole weight, that it would find it difficult to retire upon occasion.

The elbows must be almost on a line, and of an equal height, that one shoulder may not be higher than the other, and that they may be both turned alike; the left hand must be over against the top of the ear, the hilt of the sword a little above the hip, turning towards half *quart*, the thumb extended, pressing the middle of the eye of the hilt, keeping the fingers pretty close to the handle, especially the little one, in order to feel the sword firmer and freer in the hand.

By feeling the sword, is meant commanding the *fort* and *feeble* equally with the hand, in order to communicate to the more distant part of the blade, as well as to that which is nearer, the motion and action that is requisite.

The hilt should be situated in the centre, that is to say, between the upper and lower parts, and the inside and outside of the body, in order to be in a better condition to defend whatever part may be attacked. The arm must not be straight nor too much bent, to preserve its liberty and be covered. the parts being thus placed, the wrist and the point of the right foot will be on a perpendicular line.

The point of the sword ought to be about the height of, and on

PLATE 2
TOP: A LUNGE IN *QUART*
BOTTOM: A THRUST IN *QUART*

a line with the adversary's shoulder, that is, it must be more or less raised, according as he is taller or shorter: some masters raise it to one fixed height, which would be very well if all men were of the same stature; but if we consider the difference in height of persons, we shall find it evidently bad. it is to be observed, that according to the length or shortness of the blade, the line from the shell to the point is higher or lower, when the height of the point is fixed.

The shoulder, the bend of the arm, the hilt, the point of the sword, the hip, the right knee and the point of the right foot must be on a line.

The head should be upright and free without stiffness or affectation, the face turned between full and profile, and not altogether full, as many masters will have it, that being a constrained and disagreeable figure.

The sight should be fixed on the adversary's, not only to observe his motions, but also to discover his design, it being possible to guess at the interior design, by the exterior action.

It is necessary to appear animated with a brave boldness, for nothing requires a man to exert himself more than sword in hand; and it is as difficult to attain such an air of intrepidity without much exercise, as it is to become perfectly expert.

CHAPTER 3
Of Pushing Quart

To push *quart* within, besides the precautions of placing yourself to advantage, and of pushing properly and swiftly, which is to be acquired by practice and nice speculation, it is necessary that the parts, in order to assist each other in making the thrust, should be so disposed and situated, as that the wrist should draw with it the bend of the arm, the shoulder, and the upper part of the fore-part of the body, at the same time that the left hand and arm should display or stretch themselves out smartly, bending one of the knees and extending the other, which gives more vigour and swiftness to the thrust; and the body finding itself drawn forward by the swift motion of the wrist and other parts, obliges the right foot to go forward in order to support it, and to give the thrust a greater length; the left foot should, at the same instant, turn on the edge, without stirring from its place; whilst the right foot coming smartly to the ground, finishes the figure, extension and action of the lunge. This is the order and disposition of the parts in making the thrust, which see in the second plate. At the instant when the wrist moves forward, it must do three things, turn, support and oppose.

To turn the wrist in *quart*, the thumb nail must be up, and the inside edge equal in height with the other, for if it were not so high, the thrust would not be so swift, for want of motion enough, neither would the body be so well covered, because the edge, instead of being directly opposite to the adversary's sword, would fall off with a slant; and if it were higher, it would make a *quint* figure, which, by the excessive turn of the wrist, would weaken the thrust, and by the unequal turn of the edges would uncover the body.

The wrist ought to be of a height sufficient to cover the body without contracting the arm, which cannot be fixed to a particular height; for a short man against a tall one, should raise it as high as the head, which people of equal; stature, or a tall man against a short one, ought not to do.

When the opposition is accompanied with such a turn and support of the wrist as will cover the body, it is good, but if the wrist be carried too far in, you not only lose part of the length of the thrust, but also uncover the outside of the body, which are two very great faults.

The thrust must be made on the inside of the right shoulder, in order to take the *feeble* with your *fort*, and that you may be covered, bearing on the adversary's sword, by which means, the thrust will be well planted, and you less liable to receive one, which advantages you lose by pushing otherwise.

In order to make the thrust perfect, it must have its proper strength and support when planted: the strength, is the vigour with which the thrust is made, and the support is the consequence of the motion of the wrist, turning and bearing upwards, which makes the foil to bend accordingly, fixing itself until you retire.

The foil may bend upwards in two manners; the best way for it to bend, is from the middle towards the button; the other way is, when almost all the blade makes a semi-circle. The first has a better effect, the *feeble* being stronger, the other makes a greater show; but the point being *feeble*, there is not the same advantage in the thrust.

In all thrusts, the button should hit before the right foot comes to the ground, and the left hand and arm be stretched out smartly, to help the body forward, and give more swiftness to the thrust: the left hand should always be conformable to the right, turning to *quart* or *tierce*, according to the thrust. The left hand and arm should be on a line with the thigh, and their height a little lower than the shoulder.

The body must lean a little forward before, to give the thrust a greater length; the hips must not be so much bent as other times; which weakens and shortens the thrust, by the distance which the lowering the body causes from the height of the line which must come from the shoulder; besides it is harder to recover, and you, by that means, give the adversary an opportunity of taking your *feeble* with his *fort*, your situation being very low. The front of the body should be hid by turning the two shoulders equally on a line.

The foot should go out straight; in order to preserve the strength and swiftness of the thrust, it must have its proper line and distance. The line must be taken from the inside of the left heel to the point of the adversary's right foot; if it turn inward or outward, the button will not go so far, the straight line being the shortest; besides the body would be uncovered, for by carrying the foot inwards, the flank is exposed, and by carrying it outwards the front of the body, and the body is thereby weakened; the prop and the body being obliged to form an angle instead of a straight line, from the heel of the left foot to the point or button of the foil.

In order to know the distance of the lunge, the right knee being bent, must form a perpendicular line with the point of the foot; if the foot were not so forward, the heel would be off the ground, and the body would have less strength, and if it were carried farther the body could not easily bend it self, and consequently could not extend so far; moreover, it would want strength, being at too great a distance from the perpendicular line of the foot and leg, which are its support, and its recovery would be more difficult.

The foot should fall firm without lifting it too high, that the sole of the sandal, or pump, may give a smart sound, which not only looks better and animates more, but also makes the foot firm, and in a condition to answer the swiftness of the wrist.

Care must be taken not to carry the point of the foot inward or outward, because the knee bending accordingly, as part of the thigh, goes out of the line of the sword, and consequently, of the line of defence, besides it is very disagreeable to the sight.

The feet sometimes slip in the lunge, the right foot sliding forward, or the left backward; the first is occasioned by carrying out the foot before the knee is bent, whereas when the knee brings it forward, it must fall flat and firm; the other proceeds from the want of a sufficient support on the left foot.

The head should follow the figure of the body; when this is upright, that should be so to; when the body leans, the head must lean; when you push within, you must look at your adversary on the outside of your arm, which is done without turning the head, by the opposition of the hand only.

That every thrust may carry with it it's due extent and strength, the opposition of the sword, the true placing of the body, and a facility of recovering; you are to observe that the two first are for offence, and the others for defence.

Every thrust must have it's just length, and carry with it a good air, a regular situation, vigour, and a due extension—see the 2nd plate.

OF RECOVERING IN GUARD

As soon as the thrust is made, you must recover in guard, which is done either by retiring out of measure, or only to the place from whence you, pushed; if out of measure, it is done by springing back, or by bringing the right foot back behind the left, and the left behind the right; and if to the place from whence you pushed, you must parry if there's a thrust made; and if not, you must command the *feeble* of the adversary's sword, in order to cover the side on which it is, without giving an open on the other side, which is done as you recover, by drawing back the body on the left foot; which should bring with it the right knee, drawing the foot, with the heel a little raised from the ground, to prevent any accident that may happen by the badness of the terrace.

By this recovery, commanding the adversary's sword, you either get light if he not stir, or time if he does, which instead of being dangerous, as has formerly been thought, it is, by the help of art, become advantageous.

CHAPTER 4
Of the Parade of Quart

To parry, signifies, in our art, to cover when the adversary pushes, that part which he endeavours to offend; which is done it either by the opposition of the sword or of the left hand; but as I am now speaking of the sword only, I must observe; that in order to parry well with it, you are to take notice of the manner and swiftness of your adversary: by the manner, is meant whether in *quart* or *tierce*; with his *fort* to your *feeble*, or with his *feeble* to your *fort*; and you are to observe the swiftness of his thrust, that you may regulate your parade accordingly.

When a thrust is made with the *fort* to your *feeble*, which is the best way; you must, by raising and turning the hand a little in *quart*, raise the point, which brings it nearer to you, and hinders the adversary from gaining your *feeble*, which being raised up is too far from him, and makes it easy for you to seize his *feeble*—refer to the 3rd plate.

If the thrust be made on the *fort* or middle of your sword, you need only turn the hand a little in *quart*.

If after the adversary has pushed *quart*, he pushes *seconde*; you must parry with the *fort*, bringing it nearer to you, and for the greater safety, or to avoid other thrusts, or the taking time on your return, you must oppose with the left hand, which hinders him from hitting you as he meets your thrust, and from parrying it, for want of having his sword at liberty—refer to the 6th plate.

The same opposition may be made on a lunge in *quart*, and to be more safe in returning thrust or thrusts, you must close the measure in parrying, which confounds the enemy, who finds himself too near to have the use of his sword: your sword, in

PLATE 3
TOP: PARADE OF *QUART*
BOTTOM: PARADE OF *QUART* OPPOSING WITH THE HAND

PLATE 4
TOP: A LUNGE IN *TIERCE*
BOTTOM: *TIERCE* PARRIED

parrying, must carry it's point lower and more inward than in the other parades.

If the adversary makes a thrust, with shortening or drawing back his arm, or leaving his body open; you must defend with the left hand, and lunge straight on him, unless you had rather parry with the sword, making use of the opposition of the hand, and closing the measure, as I just now observed.

You may also parry in disengaging,[1] drawing back the body to the left, in order to give the hand time and facility to make the parade.

There are several other parades, of which I shall treat in their proper places, confining myself now to the most essential.

---

1. I am not of opinion that the body should be drawn back, except it be impossible to avoid the thrust without doing it; all parades being best when the body is not disordered.

CHAPTER 5

Of Pushing *Tierce* Without, or on the Outside of the Sword

In order to push *tierce* well, the hand being gone first, taking the *feeble* with the *fort*, turning down the nails, and the wrist a little outwards, not too high or low; in order not to give light above or below, the body must bend more forward and inward than in *quart*; the left hand should extend itself in *tierce*, because it ought, in all cases, to be conformable with the right, except that it is lower. When you push *tierce*, you should look within your sword: as to the feet, they must be, in every lunge, on the same line, and at the same distance.

The rules I have laid down for recovering in *quart*, will serve also in *tierce*, but of the contrary side.

PARADE OF *TIERCE*

To parry a thrust made with the *fort* to the *feeble*, you must turn the whole hand, carrying it a little outwards, raising the point, in order to avoid the adversary's taking your *feeble*, and at the same time take his—see the 4th plate.

If a thrust be made on the middle, or *fort* of your sword, you need only turn the hand, carrying all the blade equally outwards. Some masters teach to parry this thrust with the hand in *quart*, which is very dangerous if the enemy pushes *quart* over the arm in the *fort*, or *quart* within, in the *feeble*, there being an opening in one, as well as the other case; besides the point is too far from the line, to make a quick return.

To avoid the return of a thrust when you have pushed *tierce*, and

PLATE 5
TOP: PARADE OF *TIERCE* YIELDING THE *FEEBLE*.
BOTTOM: THE SAME PARADE & OPPOSITION OF THE HAND

that the adversary, in parrying, has gained to your *feeble*; you must, by raising and opposing with the *fort*, bring the pommel of your sword on high; so that the point be downwards; whereby his point will be near your left shoulder, and you, not only avoid being hit, but you may make a thrust at the same time, by opposing with the left hand, and for the greater safety, you must return on the blade, and push straight, without quitting it—see the 5th plate.

When a thrust is made in *tierce* upon the blade on the *feeble*, or by disengaging; though the first is more easily parried, you must yield the *feeble*, opposing with the *fort*, in order to guide the adversary's sword to the place the most convenient for the opposition of the left hand, and closing the measure at the same time, you have an opportunity, before he can recover, to hit him several times; which must be done by advancing on him, as fast as he retires—see the 5th plate.

You may also parry by disengaging, drawing the body back. the return is easy, by pushing *quart*; and to avoid a second thrust from the enemy at the time of your return, you must oppose with the left hand—see the 5th plate.

CHAPTER 6
Of Pushing Seconde

In pushing under, the hand must be turned in *seconde*, as high as in *quart*, and more within than in *tierce*; the body should be more bent, lower, and more forward than in thrusting *tierce*, and the left hand lower..

Seconde ought not be pushed, but on the following occasions: first, when an engagement, feint or half-thrust, is made without, that the adversary at one of these times parries high, secondly, when your adversary engages your sword on the outside, with his hand raised high; or on the inside, with his *feeble* only; and thirdly, upon a thrust or pass, within or without.

The recovery in guard, should be in *quart* within the arm, though most masters teach to recover on the outside, which takes much more time, and though the *seconde* is independent on the side, it is nearer to the inside than to the outside; because the adversary carries his wrist to the outside, when he gives an opportunity of making this thrust; therefore you ought to return to his sword in the shortest time, in order to be sooner on your guard. If you examine this parade, you will find it is the only means of recovering with safety.

What introduced the manner of returning to the sword on the outside, was the false method formerly used in parrying the *seconde* by beating on the blade; in *tierce*, with the point downwards; so that the adversary not being able to return but above, there was a necessity for returning to the sword on the outside in order to defend; but the parade and return being no longer the same, the manner of returning to the sword must also be different.

CHAPTER 7

The Parades of Seconde

Seconde may be parried three ways. First, according to the ancient manner I just described, which is done by a semi-circle on the inside, with the hand in *tierce*, the point low, almost on a line with the wrist; but the greatness of the motion does not only render it difficult to parry the thrust but still harder to parry the feint of the thrust and come up again; besides the riposte is dangerous; because it requires a long time to raise the point, which is almost as low as the ground, to the body; in which time, the adversary has not only an opportunity of parrying the thrust, but also of hitting you whilst you are bringing up your point.

Secondly, *seconde* may be parried by making a half-circle on the outside, the wrist in *quart*, as high as the shoulder, the arm extended, and the point very low—see the 6th plate. It is less dangerous, and more easy for the riposte than the former, which must be made as soon as you have parried, by pushing straight in *quart* which the adversary having pushed under, can hardly avoid, but by yielding, and battering the sword—see the 6th plate.

To this manner of parrying *seconde*, there is but one opposite, which is done by feinting below, and as the adversary is going to cross your sword, in order to parry, you must disengage by a little circle, with the hand in *seconde*, which preventing the enemy's sword, gives an opportunity of hitting him above, if the wrist is lower than I have observed, or in *flanconnade*, if the wrist is high. A man that parries below, in order to avoid this feint, must redouble his circle to meet the blade. This parade is best in recovering, after having pushed, not only to avoid the straight or low riposte, but also any feint or thrust.

The third and best parade, is made with your *fort* to the middle of the adversary's sword, the wrist turned in *quart*, but a little lower: The riposte of this parade is very good, when you know how to bind the sword upon the riposte; and it cannot be parried without returning to the parade that I have here, before, described and which, I believe, is peculiar to myself.

this parade is by so much the more advantageous, as the riposte is easy the sword being near the adversary's body, which makes it, more difficult for him to avoid you; besides, by this parade, you are in better condition to parry, not only a thrust below, but also any other thrusts and feints, the sword being near the situation of guard.

CHAPTER 8
Of Quart Under the Wrist

This thrust should not be made but instead of *seconde*, that is to say, on an engagement, parade, or lunge of the adversary in *quart*.

The wrist must not be so much turned up, nor so high as in *quart* within; the body should be more inward, and bending more forward—refer to the 6th plate.

In case the adversary pushes *quart*, in order to take the time, you must lunge the foot strong inward, to throw the body farther from the line of the adversary's sword.

In recovering from this thrust, the wrist must be in *tierce*, and the sword without the enemy's whilst the other parts take their situation.

The parade of this thrust is made by a half-circle of the sword within, the wrist raised in *quart*, and the point low—see the 6th plate.

PLATE 6
TOP: THRUST UNDER THE WRIST
BOTTOM: ITS PARADE

PLATE 7
TOP: *FLANNCONADE*
BOTTOM: THE OPPOSITION OF THE HAND TO THE LOWERING THE BODY

CHAPTER 9
Of Flanconnade

This thrust is to be made only in engaging or riposting when the adversary carries his wrist too far inward, or drops the *feeble* of his sword, then you must press a little within, and with your *feeble* on his, in order to lower it, and by that means get an opening in his flank.

The body, in this thrust, is not so straight as in *quart* within, though the arms are—see the 7th plate.

It is necessary to oppose with the left hand, in order to avoid a low thrust on your engaging, pushing or riposting. This is the last thrust of the five which are to be made in our art. The first is *quart* within the sword, the second *tierce* without the sword, the third *seconde* under the sword, the fourth *quart* under the sword, and the fifth, *flanconnade*; and there is not any attack, thrust, feint, time or riposte in this extensive art, but what depends on one of these.

The recovery from *flanconnade*, should be the same as from *quart* within the sword.

flanconnade is generally avoided by taking the time in *seconde* with the body low; the hand must oppose to shun the thrust, and hit the adversary at the same time. Instead of pushing at the flank, you should push within the body—see the 7th plate.

Besides the taking time in *seconde*, there is another very good parade, very little practised in schools; either because few masters know it, or because it is more difficult to execute it justly. This parade is made by lowering the adversary's sword, bringing it under yours to the inside, and parrying a little lower on the *feeble* of his sword, you make your riposte where he intended his thrust, that is to say in the flank.

Chapter 10
Of Parades

There are two sorts of parades, the one by binding the blade, the other by a dry beat. The binding parade is to be used when you are to riposte in *quart* within, in *tierce* without, in *seconde* under, in *flanconnade*, and in all feints: and the beat, giving a favourable opportunity of riposting, is to be used when you riposte to a thrust in *seconde*; or when after having parried a thrust in *quart* within, you see an opening under the wrist. To these two thrusts, you must riposte almost as soon as the adversary pushes, quitting his blade for that purpose, which is to be done only by a smart motion, joining again immediately, in order to be in defence if the adversary should thrust.

There are three things more to be observed in parrying. First, that you are to parry all thrusts with the inmost edge, except in yielding parades, which are made with the flat. Secondly, that your *fort* be to the middle, and your middle to the *feeble* of the adversary's sword.

And thirdly, that your situation be as rear to the guard as possible, as to favour your riposte.

THE RIPOSTES

In order to riposte well, you must observe the adversary's time and recovery in guard. The time is to be taken in the thrusts of opposition when he is recovering, and the other as soon as you have parried. There are three ways of riposting on the adversary's recovery in guard: when he does not come enough to the sword, or not at all: the second, when he comes too much, and the third, when his recovery and parade are just. To the first, you must riposte straight; to the second by disengaging, or cutting over or under, according as you see light; and to the last, by making a straight feint or half-thrust, to oblige the adversary to come to the parade, and then pushing where there is an opening, which is called baulking the parade.

CHAPTER 11
Of the Demarches, or Manner of Advancing and Retiring

Most of the faults committed in making thrusts when the measure is to be closed, proceed from the disorder of the body, occasioned by that of the feet, so that for want of moving well, you are not only in danger of being taken on your time, but likewise you cannot execute your thrusts neatly, justly, nor swiftly; the body being disordered and weak. There are ten *demarches* in fencing; four in advancing, five in retiring, and one to turn your adversary, or hinder him from turning you. The first *demarche* in advancing, is made by lifting and carrying your left-foot the length of your shoe before the right, keeping it turned as in guard, with the knee bent, lifting up the heel of the right-foot, leaning the body forward, which, on this occasion, gives it more strength and a better air; then carrying the right-foot about two foot before the left, in order to be in guard, which is done by a smart beat of the right-foot.

The same *demarche* in retiring, is made by lifting and carrying the right foot the length of the shoe behind the left, with the knee a little bent, then carrying the left-foot on the line, and to the distance of guard.

The second *demarche* is called closing the measure; which is done by lifting and advancing the right-foot a bout a foot with a beat, drawing the left the same length; because by drawing it more or less you would lose your strength or your measure, which few people have observed.

There is such a *demarche* backward, which is called breaking measure; which is done by lifting and carrying the left-foot a foot back, drawing or bringing back the right in proportion according as the ground will permit.

If the ground be uneven, or that you have a mind to surprise an unskilful man by gaining measure unperceived, or to oblige one, a little expert, to push at the time you advance your body; you must, I say, if your adversary is unskilful, bring the left-foot more or less near the right, as you are more or less out of measure, which gains more ground, and less visibly than the foregoing *demarche*, and is more favourable to your thrust: if your adversary is a little expert, and pushes on this your advancing you must bring back the left-foot to it's place, and he will be out of measure, though by means of his lunge you will be well in measure, which is a great advantage.

The same *demarche* may be made in retiring, where the ground is uneven, lifting the right-foot, bringing it near the left, and putting back the left in guard.

To make a thrust in three motions, being out of measure, you must make a double beat, which is done by a small beat of the right-foot in the same place, beginning immediately with the same foot to close the measure.

The three ways of retiring which I have shown, are done from the situation in guard. the two which are done after a lunge are, first by lifting and bringing the right-foot back from the place of the lunge behind the left, and then carrying the left behind the right, in order to be in guard.

The late Monsieur De Latouche, and Monsieur De Liancour, found this *demarche* better than the following one, though it is not so generally used.

The second retreat after having pushed, is made by drawing back the right-foot about the length of the shoe, bending the knees, in order to be in a condition to chase or drive back the left-foot with the right, keeping the hams very supple, the body free, and the sword before you; not only that you may spring the farther, but also to be in a better posture of defence. The point of the right-foot should come down first, leaning immediately after on the heel; the left-foot must fall on the line at the distance, and in the situation in guard, as I before observed, in order to be ready to take the time, or to make a riposte.

The two masters that I have quoted, condemned this retreat very much, especially Monsieur de Latouche, who says in springing back, three motions are necessary; first to draw back the right-foot in guard, secondly to bend the knee, and thirdly to chase or fly back. Any master, will find that there should be but two motions, it being easy to bend the knees and draw back the right-foot at the same time.

Besides, his rule for springing back is false; for by drawing the right-foot back so far as in guard; you lose time, the first motion being too long, and the feet being so close together, the body has not sufficient strength, and consequently cannot go far. From this it is plain that three motions are not necessary for springing back, there being but two in all. He likewise says that the leaping back, requires such an effort, that you have not power to parry; but experience sufficiently shows that you may easily parry and spring back. Indeed on a moving sand, or slippery ground, it is very difficult to leap back; and if we consider things rightly, we cannot find our purpose answered at all times and places; and though the first retreat that I recommended, and which these gentlemen esteemed, is very good, yet if you are followed closely in retreating thus, as the two steps do not place you at so great a distance, by much, as the springing back, you may be put to a nonplus by a redouble.

When you know the just length of your adversary's thrust, you may break or steal out of measure, by leaning back the body, without stirring the foot.

If in the field, you have the disadvantage of the ground, the wind, or the sun, or that in a school, you are exposed to too much light, or, pushing with an awkward man; in order to obviate these inconveniencies, you must go round him, which may be done within or without according as you have room.

The turning must be done out of measure, and with great caution: when it is within your sword, you must begin with your left-foot, carrying it to that side, and then bring the right-foot to it's proper line and distance; and if your adversary turns on the outside, you must carry the right-foot to that side, and the left in guard, as well to avoid his thrusts, as to lay hold on every favourable opportunity, in case he should persist in his *demarche*.

You should never give measure but to your inferior: giving measure, is when the body and feet advance too much, or in disorder; or advancing before you are well situated, although corrected in the *demarche*, or advancing when you are near enough, except you be much superior to the enemy.

The measure should be given to oblige the adversary to push; in order to get an opportunity of taking the time, or of riposting.

CHAPTER 12
Of Disengagements

There is nothing more nice, or more necessary in fencing, than disengagements; the nicest motion, being the smoothest and finest, and the most necessary, there being but few thrusts where you ought not to disengage, and to several more than once; and there is no better means of avoiding the advantage that a strong man has when he presses on your sword.

If we confine ourselves, strictly, to the meaning of disengagements, we shall find it to be of three sorts; which are, upon the blade, over the point, and under the wrist: but as this might be too intricate in lessons, and a learner mistake one for another; none should be called a disengagement, but that which is made on the blade; and though the others are, in effect, disengagements, especially that over the point, which is done closer than those under the wrist, yet they are distinguished from disengagements, by calling them cuts over the point, and under the wrist, according as they are used.

In order to disengage and push from the outside to the inside, being in guard towards half *quart*; the wrist must be raised a little at the time that you lower the point and raise it again, which should be done as close as possible, by a smooth and quick motion, that you may be covered and lose no time, and be able to push with your *fort* to the adversary's *feeble*.

Some people, in pushing *quart* and *tierce*, keep the wrist in *tierce*, in order to push *quart* the swifter, which is a fault; because they accustom themselves to a situation, which, when they come to assault, is unsafe and dangerous, for want of being in the guard of defence.

In disengaging from the inside to the outside, the wrist should turn a little more towards *quart*, than in the guard which I have recommended: the point should fall and rise and the same instant, and the hand should turn insensibly in *tierce*, as the thrust goes forward.

Some masters teach to hold the sword in guard between *quart* and *tierce*, and to disengage in that situation; whereby the three advantages which the disengagement in half-*quart* gives you, are lost; that is to say, first, a good air, secondly, the being covered with the *fort* of the sword, and thirdly, the swiftness of the thrust; because the hand has not a sufficient freedom of motion.

The knowing how to disengage barely is not sufficient; it is necessary that you be acquainted with the time, and with your adversary's play, in order to disengage to advantage. The time is when the adversary comes to your sword; and when your adversary, depending on his strength, comes to your blade, in order to guide his thrust to your body, is what is meant by his play or manner. You may indeed disengage without taking the time, but with less success.

When the adversary engages swift, it is good to keep your point a little low, or distant from his; by which means he requires more time to engage you, and gives you more to prevent him, unless you suffer him to touch your sword; which would not only make you lose the time of hitting him, but would also expose you to receive a thrust, it being certain that when you go to the blade on one side, you cannot defend the other; for you cannot do two opposite actions at one and the same time; and by the same rule, if you miss the time of disengaging, and disengage too late, you expose yourself to his thrust; for you cannot, at the same time, quit his blade and parry.

Though it is necessary that every Fencer should understand the disengagements, it is more especially so to tall and weak men. To the first, that they may keep their adversary at a distance; which by reason of their height, is an advantage to them; and to the others in order to prevent closing; in which case, their weakness would be a disadvantage to them.

CHAPTER 13
Of Feints

Feints are much used in fencing, whether it be by reason of their number, their ease, or the success that attends them, gaining more time and light than is to be got in plain thrusts, there being no thrust to be given so well as after a feint.

The number of feints is so great, by reason of the many guards and parades, that I should find it as difficult to describe them, as the reader would to comprehend them without experience; so that I shall confine myself to those from which the rest derive, which are, straight feint, feint, and double feint.

By straight feint, is meant a motion or feint to thrust on the side on which your sword is, which is to be done on the inside, the wrist in *quart*, a little higher than the point which must be near the adversary's sword, that you may be covered, whilst you endeavour to get an opening. This motion should be attended with a little beat of the right-foot, keeping back the body. If, at the time you feint, your adversary does not stir, you must push *quart*: if he parries with his *feeble*, you must immediately disengage to *tierce*; and if he parries high you must cut in *quart* under the wrist.

The feint, to which I give no other name, it being the most used, and to distinguish it from the others, is done by feinting from *quart* to *tierce*, with a little beat of the foot, keeping the body back: the wrist must be raised in *quart*, and the button a little lower than the pommel, near the adversary's blade; by which means you are covered, and can make your thrust swifter. If the adversary does not stir at the feint, you must go on straight with the *tierce*: if he parries with his *feeble*, you must disengage and thrust *quart*, and if he parries with his *fort*, you must push *seconde*.

Several masters teach to make this feint from the inside to the outside, with the wrist turned in *tierce*; and indeed they are seemingly in the right; a feint being a likeness of the beginning of a thrust; and that likeness cannot be better shown than in the figure of the thrust: but the smart motion of the point, causes the adversary to stir, the figure of the hand no way contributing thereto. You are to consider which is the most proper, not only to make the adversary answer you, but also to make the motion quicker. Monsieur De Latouche says, that from *quart* to *quart* there is no motion; but we have two instances to the contrary. First, that a man of experience has his wrist and the bend of his arm free, so as to thrust straight in *quart*, though in the same figure; and secondly, if there be a motion preceding the thrust, as in a disengagement, or a cut under; this motion is sufficient to help the swiftness of the feint, and of the thrust: in short, the motion from *quart* to *quart*, being quicker than feinting from *quart* to *tierce*, and returning in *quart*; it ought to have the preference, swiftness being the line of fencing. The only feints that should be made in *tierce*, are those that are marked from below above to return below, and from above below to return above.

The double feint is in two motions, so that in order to push within the sword, you must be without; and making a little motion in *quart* within, with a little beat of the foot, you feint again without closing the measure, keeping back the body in order to be out of the adversary's reach: if he parries with his *fort*, you must cut under in *seconde*, and if he parries with his *feeble*, disengage to *quart* within.

As there are in this thrust three motions of the sword, *viz.* the two feints and the thrust; the foot must make as many, in order to answer the motions of the hand.

Some masters teach to make the double feint without stirring the foot; and others teach to advance on the first motion. In the first case, being in the adversary's measure, you lose too much time, which is very dangerous: and advancing on the first motion, is almost as dangerous as keeping the foot firm, by putting yourself within the adversary's reach; besides the manner is not so graceful as that which I recommend, in which you are not within his reach until the second motion; and this is attended with another advantage; for by bearing with the right-foot, the body must of necessity be kept back, and consequently, farther from the sword of the adversary, and in a better condition to act.

There are two other ways of making these thrusts: the one by an interval between the first and second motions, joining or uniting the other two; and the latter between the second and third motions, joining the two first. Though both these methods are good, I prefer the latter, which puts you in a better condition, not only to avoid your adversary's thrust, but also to choose your own; the interval giving you a favourable opportunity of doing both.

There has been so much said of the feints which I have described, with their opposites, that I shall say no more of them, nor will I speak of an infinite number of other feints, straight, single, and double, within, without, and under, in disengaging, or cutting over the point, or under the wrist, in riposting, or redoubling thrusts; all which, depend on the three which I have described; in which, as in all thrusts, the body must be kept back, and the *fort* of the sword before you; by which means, you are more out of danger, and the wrist is better prepared. Some men mark feints with the head and body, which is a very disagreeable sight, and dangerous with regard to time.

A feint is the likeness of the beginning of a thrust: it is made to put the adversary off his guard, and to gain an opening. In order to take advantage of the time and light which you get by your feint, you must take care to avoid an inconveniency into which many people fall, by uncovering themselves in endeavouring to uncover the adversary.

CHAPTER 14

Of Cutting Over the Point of the Sword

In order to cut over the point, within from without, the wrist must be turned towards *tierce*, which gives it a swifter motion. When your point is over your adversary's, you must turn the wrist in *quart*, pushing with your *fort* to his *feeble*: though this is a regular way of cutting, what is most essential to perfect the thrust is wanting, that is to say, the motion that should precede it, which is commonly a half-thrust or feint, by which, two advantages are gained: first you discompose your adversary, and secondly, your thrust is swifter, being by so much the more vigorous, as the motion previous thereto is so. At the time you make a half-thrust or feint, you must make a little beat with the foot, bearing back the body to break your Adversary's measure.

The cut from the inside to the outside, has commonly more success than that from the outside to the inside, the adversary going more readily to his parade on this side than on the other. The manner of cutting on the outside, is by placing your sword within, making a little motion or straight feint, the wrist in *quart*, the *fort* of the sword before you, in order to be covered, and your point very near the adversary's sword; you must beat a little with the foot, bending the body back a little, and as the adversary is going to parry with the *feeble*, you must pass your point quickly over his, pushing in *tierce*, with your *fort* to his *feeble*.

Though all thrusts have the same following ones; the cut has them more easy; it's motion from above to below, disposing it better than the disengagements, if the thrust be from the outside to the inside, and that the adversary parries with his *fort* to your *feeble*: besides the recovery in guard, which is common after all thrusts, you must, upon a parade with the *fort*, if it be without stirring the foot, or in advancing, join: and if the adversary makes this parade in retiring, he gives you an opportunity of cutting in *quart* under the wrist, and on his parrying with the *feeble*, you must return in *seconde*, bringing forward the left-foot a little, in order to procure a reprise or second lunge.

These two reprises are to be made before you are acquainted with your adversary's manner of parrying; but when you have discovered it, if it be with his *fort*, you must cut over and under the wrist in *quart*, and if with his *feeble*, return in *tierce*, that is to say, make an entire circle. These cuts are to be made in one or two motions; in the first you are not to stop, but in the other, you make a short interval by a little beat with the foot.

The thrusts following the cut from the inside to the outside, before you know your adversary's parade, are made thus: if it is with the *fort*, you must return with a cut in *seconde*, under the sword, advancing the left-foot a little; if he parries with the *feeble*, you must return by disengaging to *quart* within, advancing the left-foot, as before: some people return a cut in *tierce*, in *quart*, by another cut over the point, of *quart* in *tierce*, and so on the contrary side.

When you foresee the parade, you may at once cut from the inside to the outside, and under in *seconde*; or return within, according as the parade is made with the *fort* or *feeble*. You may also make these redoubles by a little interval over the sword, beating with the foot.

There are other redoubles which are made by drawing back the body without stirring the feet.

See the chapter of reprises.

The cut may be made not only after a half-thrust, or straight feint, as I have said, but also after an engagement, lunge, or pass, and in riposting, which is the best and most used; because that is to be done only in recovering to guard, or by bringing one foot behind the other, or springing back; to the first you must riposte with the foot firm, and to the other by closing the measure.

Chapter 15
Of the Reprise, or Redoubled Thrust

The term reprise signifies a succession of thrusts without interval, or with very little. it may be done in three manners; first after having pushed without recovering, secondly, in recovering or being recovered; and thirdly, when the enemy steals measure.

The first and last of these three reprises may be called redoubles.

The first reprise is made after having pushed *quart*, the enemy having parried with his *feeble*, you must return in *seconde*, advancing the left foot a little to make the action easier to the right foot, and though it be not necessary to advance it unless the enemy retires, it serves for an ornament, and to give more vigour to the thrust: but if as soon as the enemy has parried he ripostes, you must only redouble with the hand, the body low without stirring the feet, and join. If he ripostes under the wrist in the flank, you must either parry crossing his sword as you recover, opposing with the left hand, or return, as I said, with the hand in *seconde*.

Upon the riposte of the enemy, you may also redouble, *volting* straight, or cutting in the flank according as he raises his hand more or less in his riposte, in order to facilitate your *volt*; you must immediately after your lunge follow a little with the left foot.

The second reprise is made, after having pushed *quarte*, when in recovering to guard the enemy advances, without being covered, or that suffering the superiority of your sword, he gives you room to thrust in *quarte*, if he disengages, you must go off in *tierce*, if he forces your sword with his *feeble*, you must disengage to *tierce*, and if with his *fort* cut *quarte* under the wrist.

In order to get time for this redouble, you must make a half thrust, immediately getting out of measure, either with the body simply, or by the first *demarche* backwards, or by leaping a little back; if the enemy advances it will be either straight or making a feint, or on your sword; to the two first you must push straight *quarte*, or *seconde*, lowering the body or *volting*, and if he comes on your sword you must disengage and push over in *tierce*.

The third reprise is made when the enemy upon your pushing *quarte* breaks measure without or with parrying; to the one you must redouble in *quarte*, with your *fort* to his *feeble*, which is done after a straight thrust, feint, engagement, or riposte; and if the enemy parries, you must likewise redouble forwards by a disengagement, or a cut under or over according to his parade, or as opportunity offers. To redouble forward, or make several reprises following with ease, you must as often as you thrust follow with the left foot.

THE REPRISES ON THE OUTSIDE

If you push in *tierce* and your adversary parries with the *fort*, you must redouble in *seconde*, and if he parries with the *feeble* disengage to *quarte*, advancing a little the left foot that the right may have the liberty of a second motion.

If the enemy after parrying *tierce* should riposte straight or under, to the first you may disengage and *volt*, and to the other *volt* straight, advancing the left foot a little in lunging, in order to have the liberty of *volting*, because you cannot easily do it when you are extended: it is more easy to take the time opposing with the left hand; and it is best of all to parry and thrust straight in *quarte*; if after having pushed *tierce*, on your recovery to guard, you find you have the command of the enemy's sword, or that he advances uncovered, you, must in these cases push straight in *tierce* if he disengage you must take the time and push *quarte*, if he comes to your sword with his *fort*, you must cut under in *seconde*, if with his *feeble*, disengage in *quarte*, it is also good after having pushed *tierce* to recover with your sword high, giving light under, and if the enemy pushes there, you must take the time opposing with the left hand, or parry and riposte.

It is good likewise for a decoy to make a half thrust and recover with the sword quite distant from you body, and if the enemy comes to your sword, you must disengage and thrust at his open, and if he makes at your body, you must *volt* or oppose with the hand and thrust where you have light.

The reprises or redoubles in advancing are made in *tierce* by the same rules as those within are. That is to say, either straight, or by disengaging or cutting over or under, according as the enemy either lets you make your thrust, or goes to his parade.

All these redoubles may be made on a riposte as well as on other lunges.

CHAPTER 16
Of Passing Quarte Within the Sword

A pass is contrary to a *volt* as well in figure as in it's occasion, the left leg in the figure passing foremost, and in a *volt* behind, to help the body to turn, and in it's occasion, the pass being to be made as in a lunge, taking the time, or his time, whereas the *volt* cannot be made without a great deal of time; yet the pass is different from a lunge, the one being made with the foremost foot, and the pass with the hindmost, which gives the thrust a greater length, more strength and swiftness, and a greater facility of taking the *feeble* with your *fort*, the body goes further, because the centre from which it departs in a lunge is in the left foot, and in a pass in the right foot which is more advanced, and also because in passing you advance the left foot more than you do the right in lunging, and the parts being higher on a pass than in a lunge there is a greater facility of taking the *feeble* with your *fort*.

In a pass in *quarte*, the hands and arms must be displayed as in a lunge, not only in their figure, but in the same order, that is to say, the hand must move first to bring on the shoulder and the body; which should lean more forward than in lunging, at the time that carrying the left foot about two foot and an half, you find your pass at it's full extension. As your body is too much abandoned forward to recover itself easily, you must rush on your enemy, seize the guard of his sword, and present him your point, which is done by advancing the right foot to such a distance as to be out of the reach of his leg whilst you advance, which otherwise might give him an opportunity, by tripping to throw you down. As you advance the right foot you must seize the guard of his sword, at the same time drawing back your sword, keeping it high. Then you must carry

PLATE 8
TOP: A PASS IN *QUART*
BOTTOM: THE LOWERING THE BODY ON THE PASS

your right foot behind the left to almost the distance of a lunge, in order to be strong, as well to avoid his pulling you forward, as to draw him to you.

If the enemy parries the pass with his *fort*, you must only join, commanding his sword with your *fort*, until you have seized his guard with the left hand, which must be done at the time that you advance the right foot, carrying your sword from the inside to the out, then you must bring the left foot to the side of the right, and bring back the right presenting the sword to the enemy.

If he parries with his *feeble*, you must, without stopping, either cut over his point from within to without, or turn the wrist in *seconde*, lowering your body, and bringing up the right foot seize his guard, then carrying your sword from within to without, you advance the left foot to the side of the right, and drawing back the right present your sword.

The easiest means to avoid and hit a man who passes in *quart* within are to parry dry and riposte swiftly in the flank, and if the pass is made straight along the blade with the *fort* to your *feeble*, you must by lowering your *feeble*, turn your wrist in *quarte* carrying the point perpendicularly down, supporting the wrist, without, and bringing your sword round by the outside of the adversary's shoulder, you find your sword above his, with your point to his body. You may also upon the same pass lower the body and push *seconde*.

To pass in *TIERCE*

In passing *tierce*, as in a lunge, the wrist must draw the shoulder and body forward, bringing, as in a pass in *quarte*, the left-foot about two feet and an half before the right, then advancing the right foremost and out of the reach of the enemy's; you must seize the guard of his sword, and again advancing the left-foot near the right, you draw back the right and present the point.

The counters or opposites to this pass, are the straight riposte, or the riposte under, the taking time, cutting *seconde* under, disengaging, or counter disengaging and *volting*, but the surest is to loosen the right-foot turning the body half round to the right, opposing with the sword and presenting the point to the enemy, which hindering him from hurting you, throws him on your

PLATE 9
TOP: THE TURNING THE BODY ON A PASS IN *TIERCE*
BOTTOM: PASS IN *SECONDE VOLTING* THE BODY

point if he abandons himself, and at the same time you seize the guard of his sword—see the 9th plate.

TO PASS IN *SECONDE*

In passing *seconde*, there must, as in a lunge, be a preparatory motion, which is made by a feint, or by an engagement on the blade to oblige the enemy to parry high, in order to take that time to pass under, which is done by advancing the left-foot very much, with the body lower and more forward than in other passes, and advancing the right-foot, you seize the enemy's sword, bringing yours from under over, and advancing the left-foot to the side of the right, you draw back the right presenting the point. You must take notice, that in a pass in *quarte* with it's joining, there are but three steps, and that in the passes in *tierce* and *seconde* there are four. The first, passing the left-foot before the right; the second, advancing the right to seize the sword; the third, bringing up the left-foot a little, and the fourth, bringing back the right, presenting the point.

In order to avoid, and to hit the enemy on his pass, besides parrying and pushing straight, as in the thrust lunged in *seconde*, you may also make a straight thrust, opposing with the left-hand, or by *volting*, as is shown in the 9th plate.

Though a pass carries along with it, as I have observed, a greater extension and swiftness than a lunge, yet as you cannot recover from it, it should be seldom practised, especially if you are not the strongest, or able in three attacks to hit twice, there being nothing more disagreeable to the sight than to see several passes made without hitting. But it is otherwise in lunges, by reason of the liberty of recovering and parrying.

Passes were more used formerly than they are now, whether it was to endeavour to bring them to perfection, or because it has been found that this sort of play was not so sure.

CHAPTER 17
Of Volting the Body

The *volting* of the body, which many people call *quarting*, should never be done but at times when you are abandoned, as in case of lunges or on an engagement of feint in disorder, of when finding yourself so disordered as not being able to parry, you must of necessity have recourse to *volting* in order to avoid the thrust; but to do it at an improper time, as some do, is very dangerous, by reason of the facility of parrying it, it being a figure in fencing which gives the least strength, extension, of swiftness to a thrust; besides that presenting the flank and small of the back, the adversary, in order to hit these parts, has nothing to do but parry with his point a little within and low.

In *volting* you must begin with the arms and left-foot, by whose assistance you turn the body; the hands should turn in *quarte*, the right as in a lunge or pass, and the left more without; you must at the same time turn upon the point of the right-foot, bringing the heel outwards, and the left-foot behind the right, a little farther outwards, which gives the body almost the figure of a left-handed man; having turned about a quarter round, the body in this posture must necessarily be in disorder—see the 9th plate.

Having finished these motions, if you find, for want of the enemy's having sufficiently abandoned himself, that you have not an opportunity of joining, you must without stirring the body or left-foot, return with your sword on the enemy's, and from his sword to his body, and from the body to the sword, as often as you shall see proper, which may be easily done, your thrusts being but of small extension, as well by reason of the action of the enemy coming to you, as by the advancement of the *volt*; you should, at the same time, oppose with the left-hand, to avoid the thrusts that the enemy might make upon the time of yours; by this means you may easily come to guard again, or if he retires you may push at him, the left-foot by it's advancement having given a great advantage to your thrust, and if instead of retiring, he has a mind to join, you must prevent him by seizing the guard of his sword, presenting your point to him.

If in an assault the foil be entangled in the shirt or elsewhere, or that in battle the sword be too far entered, or that the enemy lay hold on the blade; in these cases you must shift your sword to the other hand, which is done after the *volt*, advancing your right-foot, taking hold of your blade with the left-hand about four inches from the guard, whilst with the right you seize his guard, and drawing back your sword you present him the point.

Though *volting* is not best in combat, yet it may on some occasions be necessary, besides it is my business to speak of them, at the same time advising that it is much better to make use of parades and ripostes, than of time of what sort soever.

The joining on a *volt* is the same as on passing in *quarte*.

CHAPTER 18

Of Joining or Seizing the Sword

You may join after having parried any thrust or pass whatever, as also after having pushed, passed, or *volted* in whatever figure, or on whatever side it may be, especially when the enemy abandons himself, or you abandon yourself: if the enemy abandons himself by a lunge or pass; in case of the first, you must close the measure in parrying, seizing at the same time the guard of his sword with your left-hand and carrying the right-foot back present him the point; and in case of a pass, you must parry with your feet firm, and seize his guard, drawing back the right-foot and presenting your point in like manner. If you have pushed being too near, that your right-foot slipped, or that the enemy in parrying closed measure; if he parried with his *feeble* you must redouble in *seconde* and join, and if with his *fort*, you must oppose his sword with yours until with your left-hand you have seized the guard, advancing the left-foot; this motion being done, you pass your sword over the enemy's from within to without; and loosing the right-foot present him your point.

Upon the parade of *tierce* with the *fort*, being near you must join, seizing the guard, advancing the left leg, and drawing back the right, and present the point; or you may, before you join, cut under in *seconde*; the first is surer at the sword, and the other more beautiful in an assault where a thrust is more esteemed, than joining.

If on a pass or lunge the enemy should attempt to join or seize your sword, you must, in order to prevent him, change it from the right-hand to the left, four inches from the guard, as I have already observed, seizing his with the right-hand, and presenting him the point, holding it at such a length as to hit him whilst he is unable to come near you.

155

PLATE 10
TOP: THE SEIZING AND PRESENTING THE SWORD
BOTTOM: PARRYING AND DISARMING

In joining, if you cannot seize the guard, you must the blade, helping with your elbow, turning the hand to break the blade, or take away the sword, which may be done if you are cunning and nervous, especially if the enemy's wrist is in *quarte*, in which there is no danger of hurting yourself, because the sword cannot slip through, and consequently, can't cut your fingers, as has happened to some by their imprudence; by this means, you have time not only to secure yourself, but also to hit your enemy. some people seize the arm, but that is of no use, because the enemy may change hands and hit you.

You may throw a man down after having pushed, either upon the pass of *quarte* or *tierce*; if in *quarte*, it is done after advancing the left-foot, crossing the enemy's sword with your *fort*, and carrying your right-leg without his, at the same time pushing the sword up from the inside to the out, and carrying the right arm to his neck, and the left to the small of his back: these three actions must be done at the same time. There has been so much said on this head, with the joining without, that I shall say no more of it.

The joining in passes within, without, and under, is the same as in their lunges.

In whatever manner you join you must present the sword at a distance, in order to hinder the enemy from seizing it, or putting it off with his left hand to throw himself in upon you: if the enemy should make a difficulty of yielding up his sword, you must, in order to frustrate his hopes of closing you, and to make him follow you, draw back the left-foot behind the right, and the right behind the left, at such a distance as to be strong, at the same time moving the point of your sword circularly; by this means, you are in a condition either of giving or taking his life, which you would not be if he could close you, by which you would be obliged to kill him, or render the advantage doubtful by struggling.

CHAPTER 19
Of Engaging in *Quarte* in a Middling Guard

I have hitherto treated of the means whereby to make thrusts, and in this and the following chapters, I will show on what occasion they are to be made use of. Though there is an infinite number of figures or postures, and that every posture may be in guard, whether within, or without, *prime, seconde, tierce,* or *quarte,* they proceed from the middling guard, the straight, the high, or the low guard, each of which may be attacked and defended within or without.

Though there are many means to disorder the enemy by putting him out of guard in order to hit him on that occasion, they all depend either upon a feint by the side of his sword to draw him on, or on a motion of your sword on his, to uncover him, taking his sword from the line of your body, and placing yours on a line with his, which is called engaging. And there are several other ways of coming to the sword, which are the beats, crossings, bindings, and lashings; the occasions of which, and the manners of using them, I shall show in their proper places. I begin with engaging in the middling guard, as the neatest, the most used, and the best.

To engage this guard within, it must be done with the edge on the same side, without going wide, in order to keep your *fort* before you, and your point before the enemy, carrying both parts alike; the engagement must be made *feeble* to *feeble,* a little more to your enemy's than your own, because if it were with the *feeble* to the *fort,* the enemy's sword would not be displaced, besides if he should push, you could not parry, being unable with your *feeble* to resist his *fort*; and if it were with the *fort* to the *feeble*, you would be in danger of being hit under, where there would be an opening; besides you would be obliged to advance much, which would be dangerous.

On your engagement, the enemy may do three things, either of which, produces several others. First, either he will let you engage, or secondly, he will disengage, or thirdly, he will come to your blade.

If he lets you engage, you must push *quarte*, or, by way of precaution, make a half-thrust, in order to see if he stirs, to retire, or to have recourse to his parade, or to time.

If he does not stir, you must, as I said, push *quarte*; if he retires, redouble your thrust; if he parries with his *fort* cut *quarte* under the wrist; if with the *feeble*, disengage, or cut over the point in *tierce*; and if upon the half-thrust he takes the time pushing straight, you must parry and riposte, or take the time in *seconde*, with your body low; if he takes the time lowering his body, you must parry and oppose with the left-hand, riposting in *quarte*; if he takes the time cutting under the wrist, you must parry crossing the sword in *quarte*, opposing with the hand, in order to make your riposte more safely; and if he volts upon the half-thrust, you must parry and riposte in *flanconnade*, or take the time, with, your body low.

If when you engage he disengages, it will be either, 1st, without Design, or 2nd, to disengage and push *tierce* over, or 3rd, disengage breaking measure, or 4th, disengage, and come to your blade without, or 5th disengage making a feint, and pushing *quarte* or 6th, disengage to take a counter to your time.

1st. If he disengages with a design only to disengage, you must on the time push *tierce*.

2nd. If he disengages breaking measure, you must redouble in *tierce*, advancing.

3rd. If he disengages and pushes without, you must parry and riposte quick where you have light, or take time against him, disengaging and *volting*, or lowering the body.

4th. If he disengages and comes to your blade without; if it is with his *fort*, you must cut under in *seconde*; and if with the *feeble*, you must counter-disengage from without to within.

5th. If on the engagement, he feint *tierce* in order to push *quarte*, you must push or take the time straight upon the feint, or by lowering the body on the thrust.

6th. If he disengages giving light, to take a counter to your thrust, whether by a riposte or time, you must make a false-time or half-thrust, and if he parries, or takes the time, in case of the first, you must baulk his parade; and if he takes the time, you must take another upon him.

If, upon the engagement, he goes to your blade with his *fort*, you must cut under his wrist, and if with his *feeble*, disengage and push without in *tierce*.

Though an engagement may be made blade to blade, without disengaging, that is inside to inside; better and more common to make it by disengaging from the outside to the inside.

CHAPTER 20

Of Engaging in Tierce
in the Middling Guard

The engagement without should be made from your being placed within, *feeble* to *feeble*, for the same reason as in *quarte*, the wrist should be turned in *tierce*; in this engagement as in *quarte*, the antagonist may do three things. 1st, let you engage him, 2nd. or disengage, 3rd. or come to your blade.

If he lets you engage him, you must carry on your thrust in *tierce*, or make a half-thrust, to see if he does not stir, if he retires, if he parries, or if he takes the time.

If upon your half-thrust he does not stir, you must thrust straight, if he retires, advance and redouble.

If he parries with his *fort*, cut *seconde* under, if with his *feeble*, you must disengage or cut over the point from *tierce* to *quarte*, and if upon the half-thrust he takes the time pushing straight, you must either parry and riposte, or make him time, *volting* or lowering the body.

If he takes the time in *seconde*, lowering his body, you must either parry him and thrust *quarte*, or pushing *quarte*, oppose with the left hand, or *volt*.

If on your engagement he disengages, it is as in *quarte*, 1st either without design, 2nd. or to retire, 3rd. or to take the time pushing *quarte* or *volting*, 4th. or to come to your blade, 5th. or to make a feint; 6th. or to take a counter to your thrust.

1st. If he disengage without design, you must push straight in *quarte*, or make a half-thrust, and go on with the same.

2nd. If he disengages breaking measure, you must come forward redoubling in *quarte*.

3rd. If he disengages and pushes *quarte*, which, on this occasion, is called counter-disengaging, you must either parry and riposte, or take the time lowering the body, or *volting*.

4th. If he disengages and comes to your sword within, with his *fort*, you must cut *quarte* under the wrist, and if with his *feeble*, you must counter-disengage from the inside to the outside.

5th. If he makes a feint in order to return in *tierce*, you must either parry or take the time as I have said.

6th. If he disengages giving light, to take a counter on your thrust, whether by riposte or time, you must make a feint, and if he parries with his *fort* you must cut under in *seconde*, if with his *feeble*, you must disengage and push *quarte*, if he takes the time straight, you must lower the body, if he takes time lowering his body, you must parry and push straight in *Quarte*, if he cuts in flank, you must parry crossing the sword in *quarte*, and if he volts, you must parry and riposte in *flanconnade*.

If on the engagement without, he comes to your sword with his *fort*, you must cut under in *seconde*, if with his *feeble*, disengage or cut over the point in *quarte*.

When you are engaged within the Sword

If the Enemy engage you within with his *fort*, you must cut under the wrist, and if with his *feeble*, disengage from within to without, of if you don't care to do that, make a feint without; if on this feint he goes to the parade with his *fort*, you must push *seconde* under, and if with his *feeble*, disengage in *quarte*.

When the enemy engages to make you push, in order to parry and riposte, you must, as I have said, make a half-thrust and retire giving light, in order to take him by a counter to his thrust, by a parade, or by time.

You may on the same engagement, remain engaged on purpose, in order to make the adversary path straight; and in this case, you must parry and riposte where he is uncovered, or take time lowering the body.

If after having engaged you he should make a feint, you must, by going to the parade, give light on purpose, and if he pushes, take him by a contrary.

If he engages to make you disengage, in order to take the time on your disengagement, you must disengage and give him a little light, and if he pushes at it, take him by a riposte, or a time opposite to his.

If you are engaged in *tierce* with the *fort*, you must cut under the wrist in *seconde*, and if with the *feeble*, and the hand in *quarte*, disengage to *quarte* within, or, by way of caution, make a half-thrust; if the adversary goes to the parade, you must push where you have light, and if he takes the time, parry and riposte, or take a time to his.

You may also upon an engagement in *tierce*, make a feint below, and if he takes the time, parry above and riposte below. This thrust is very good against a man that's disordered, who coming to the parade above, gives room to hit him below.

CHAPTER 21
Of Several Guards, and the Manner of Attacking Them

Though all the guards are good when well defended, yet they are not equally good; because we ought not to look upon any thing as good, that does not procure us some advantage, and an ill placed guard, instead of being favourable, requires a great deal of skill to be of any use at all, being farther from a posture of defence, the middling guard only carrying with it such a disposition of the point and wrist as is sufficient to defend the inside, the outside, the upper and lower parts of the body with the sword: for as to the other guards, whether flat, high, or low, or holding the sword with both hands, they leave some part uncovered, either by reason of their height, or their line.

TO ATTACK A STRAIGHT GUARD

No man of skill or reason will give a considerable open without a design, and as the people who hold such a guard as I am going to describe, have their several designs, you must be cautious of them, in order not only to make them useless to them, but advantageous to yourself.

Some men hold their swords straight or flat, whether it is because they are more used to disengagements than parades, or to take advantage of the superiority of their stature, or of the length of their sword, to avoid the attacks and engagements to which the other guards are more exposed; for you can hardly engage or feint on this guard, the point being too low; so that to attack him, you must bind the sword, which you must do after placing yourself within his sword, binding his blade under yours, when he is out of measure, to take, with more ease, the *feeble* of his sword, crossing it with yours, raising your hand in *seconde*, and carrying the point low, whilst gaining measure, you form a little circle with the two points, and raising them up again, you push *seconde* within, with the body low.

Though it be almost impossible for the enemy to disengage, when you have bound his sword as I have described, it may happen that if some of the circumstances were wanting, he might disengage and push, which ought not to hinder you from making your thrust; because your sword may very well hit him, passing under his, which cannot hurt you, because of the lowness of your body.

The binding is easy to be parried, by reason of the natural tendency to follow the sword, which is done by raising and bringing your *fort* nearer. These following have commonly more success.

The first is made after having bound the sword, instead of pushing *seconde* within, you must, upon the parade, disengage and push *tierce* over: If the adversary is quick enough in his parade to shun this double motion, you must have recourse to the third, binding the sword in the like manner, and feinting above, return below.

Though the sword is seldom bound on the outside, upon some occasions and to some people it would not be amiss; it must be done with your *feeble* to the enemy's, with the precautions necessary in binding within, by a little circle without, the hand in *quarte*, and if he does not stir, or if he disengages, you must push without, the hand in *quarte*. These following are according to the parade with the *fort* or with the *feeble*, pushing *seconde* under, or *quarte* within.

As in all thrusts the hand must be easy and uniform, it must be more so in this than in the others, because the binding cannot be made without a very close and smooth motion.

Though several masters teach to disengage in order to bind the sword, I would not have it done so for two reasons: first, because the disengaging gives time to the opponent, not only to thrust straight, but also to disengage; and secondly, because you cannot so easily bind the sword as when you are on the same side.

In binding the blade, you must close the measure; because a man who is superior to you, in height, by the length of his sword, or by his situation, won't let his inferior into measure; in one or the other case, being at a proper distance, you bind more easily on the *feeble*.

PLATE 11
TOP: ATTACK IN THE HIGH GUARD
BOTTOM: ATTACK IN THE LOW GUARD

To attack the high guard

In this guard, you must place yourself under, with the hand in *seconde*, covering the upper part, in order to oblige the enemy to go under; which being the most distant place from his sword, procures you more time to avoid him. He may, on this occasion, do three things: let you engage him, go under, or force your sword.

If he lets you engage him, it is either with a design to parry, or to take the time; wherefore, before you push, you must make a half-thrust under: if he parries, it will be in one of the three ways that I have shown in the parade of *seconde*, chapter 8, where you may see all their counters.

If upon the half-thrust he takes the time, you must parry and riposte below, or push straight, opposing with the hand; you may also *volt* on this occasion, but it is better to parry.

If he opposes with his hand upon your half-thrust, you must parry with your left-hand, and, pushing near his left shoulder, baulk his hand. And if he volts on your half-thrust, you must parry and riposte in the flank.

If on the engagement he thrust under, you must parry and thrust straight, or take the time, opposing with your hand, and if instead of going under, he only feints there in order to return above; you must either parry the feint and riposte under, or push on the time, as I have said before.

If he makes use of the same thrust, pushing at the time of your going under, you must make believe to push there, returning quickly to the parade above, and riposte under.

And if he would draw you on in order to make this riposte on you, you must make a half-thrust, keeping on your parade below, to riposte straight in *quarte*.

If upon your engagement he forces your sword, you must yield the *feeble*, opposing with the *fort* and the left-hand—see the 5th plate.

To keep the enemy from forcing your sword, you must cross his blade with your *fort* to his *feeble*.

To attack the low guard

Those who hold a low guard have a design either to parry with the sword or with the hand, to lower the body or to *volt*; therefore as in the other guards you must make a false time, or half thrust, and if he parries with the sword, thrust where you see light, if he parry with the hand, you must feign a straight thrust in order to bring his left-hand to the parade, at the same time raising your point with a little circle, pushing at the left side with the hand in *seconde*, the body low, whereby you baulk his left-hand, and for the greater safety, you must oppose his thrust with your hand, endeavouring in your ripostes, to deceive his sword and his hand.

If he waits for your thrust in order to lower the body or to *volt*, you must make a half-thrust to draw him on, and take one of the counters which I have spoken of before.

If the low guard is within your sword, you must attack it making a semi-circle with the point of the sword down, lashing and crossing his, the hand in *quarte*, and to push without danger, you must oppose with the left-hand: this thrust is good against a man that pushes at the same time.

If the low guard is without your sword, you must lash in *tierce*, crossing the sword and push without.

If the low guard is neither within nor without, you must lash smartly in *tierce* and in *quarte*, that is to say on his outside and inside, pushing *quarte* afterwards, opposing with the left-hand: this thrust puzzles a man who disengages quick, which in this case is of no use.

You may also engage this guard placing yourself within, the wrist in *tierce*, and the point low (see the 11th plate) closing the enemy pretty near to oblige him to push above, and if he pushes there, you must parry and riposte above, or under, according as you have light.

If instead of making a thrust above, he makes a feint there and pushes within, or under, you must push *quarte*, opposing with the left-hand, or else going to the parade with the sword to all thrusts and feints without, leave to the left-hand the defence of the inside, and of the under part.

And if instead of pushing, he waits for your thrust to take the time upon it, you must press close upon him and push straight in *quarte*, with the point low, opposing with the left hand, in order to throw off his sword, or push at his arm, of which you are in reach, though he is not in measure of your body.

These sorts of guards are not so much practised, with sword in hand, as the middling guard, people being more careful of parrying with the sword, and a man is in much better condition to parry from the middling guard than from any other.

TO ATTACK THE GUARD WHERE THE
SWORD IS HELD IN BOTH HANDS

Those who hold the sword in both hands, that is to say, the handle in the right-hand, and the blade about four fingers breadth in the left, will either engage, or beat on your sword, with great force, or stick to a strong parade, in order to uncover you the more, in favour of their thrust.

But as they cannot keep this situation without exposing their body very much, which is often dangerous, as also a very unseemly posture, this guard is therefore, with good reason, condemned by most, if not all, experienced masters.

If you have to do with one that holds this guard, you must keep your point a little low, and be always ready to change, in order to render the strength which the left-hand gives to the right, useless, in his engaging or beating.

If he will not attack you, but waits for your thrust in order to parry and riposte, you must make a half-thrust, and recover quickly to your parade, to avoid his riposte; wherein, throwing back his left-hand, and abandoning himself extremely, he is not in a condition to avoid your thrust after you have parried his.

You may also make a home-thrust on him, by a single or double feint, because these require two or three parades; so that your adversary being unable to parry without throwing his point a great way off, he cannot bring it back in time if you disorder him by a feint.

You may likewise catch him, by placing your sword along his, with your point a little raised, and sliding on a defence along his sword, push at his left-hand or arm, for he cannot, though he goes to his parade, hinder your blade from sliding so as to hit him there, without running any risk, you being in measure of his hand and arm, when he is out of reach of your body.

You are to observe, that in all guards with sword in hand, you must push at the nearest and most uncovered part; which in the guards that I have described is the arm; therefore you must not abandon yourself to hit the body, but in riposting, or after having disordered, or engaged the enemy as aforesaid.

CHAPTER 22
Of Left-Handed Men

Most people imagine that a left-handed man has, by nature, the advantage of a right-handed man in fencing, whereas he has it only by habit, exercising oftener with right-handed men than a right-handed man with him, as well in lessons as in assaults, most masters being right-handed, as well as most of the scholars, taking lessons from the right-hand, and practising seldom with left-handed men, find themselves puzzled, nothing surprising more than what one is not used to, which is so true, that to embarrass a left-handed man, who has not fenced much, you must put another against him; I say one that has not fenced much, because right or left-handed men who go to the school of a perfect master, will be taught to use both hands, by which means, they will not be so much surprised when they meet with a left-handed man, as they would otherwise be.

When a right and a left-handed man fence together, the right handed man should push but seldom within, that being the antagonist's strongest part; and his weakest and outward, which should be kept covered, or in a defensive condition, as the most liable to be attacked; the best way is to push *quarte* without, engagements, feints under, and thrusts above, and double feints, finished above or under the wrist in *quarte*, cuts over the point without, and upon the parade, with the *fort*, or with the *feeble*, redoubling *quarte* under the wrist, or *seconde* over: these are chiefly the thrusts which a right-handed and a left-handed man may make against each other, whether on an attack, or in defence, by time or ripostes.

Several masters puzzle their scholars by telling them that with a left-handed man they must act quite contrary to what they do with a right-handed, which appears to be false; because to a right or left-handed man you must push, opposing with the sword, which is to be done by pushing *quarte*, when the enemy is within your sword, and *tierce*, when he is without. All the difference between a right and a left-handed man is, that two right, or two left-handed men, are both within or without, whereas a right with a left-handed man, the one is within when the other is without, the one in *quarte*, the other in *tierce*.

CHAPTER 23
Of the Parade of the Hand

There are, in fencing, three parades with the left-hand: the first, like the opposition that is from the top to the bottom; the second, with the palm of the hand without, towards the right shoulder, and the third, from the bottom to the top, with the outside of the hand: of these three parades, the first is the easiest, the most used, and the least dangerous: they are condemned by able men, as weakening those of the sword; wherefore it is wrong in a master to show them to a scholar, before he has practised those of the blade a good while, which being longer, can return to all feints, which the left-hand cannot, it being impossible to parry with it except you be near, which is very dangerous, as well by reason of the difficulty of meeting properly with the sword, as of the facility of deceiving the hand, which in this case has not time to come to the parade, because of it's small distance; and besides the facility of deceiving it, you need only push at the arm, sword in hand, in order to make it useless.

OF THE OPPOSITION OF THE HAND

Many people make no distinction between the parade and opposition of the hand, though there is a very great difference, the parade being made only against the adversary's thrust, and the opposition to prevent a following thrust after having parried with the sword, which is very necessary in most thrusts, especially in the ripostes which may be made to your thrust in *seconde*.

Besides the opposition of the hand, after having parried with the sword, you may oppose with it, taking the time, that is to say, when the enemy pushes from above to below, as the motion of his sword is greater than yours, having only a straight line to push *quarte* on, whereas his from above to below, is crooked, so that pushing upon his time, he cannot avoid the thrust, and you may easily oppose his with the left-hand, which is very different from the parade with the hand, to which you do not push until after you have parried.

CHAPTER 24
Of the Beat of the Foot, in Closing the Measure, or in the Same Place

Though it may seem to many people, that the beat of the foot, in gaining measure, making *appels*, or *alurements*, engagements, or other thrusts, is rather ornamental than necessary; nevertheless, there is nothing puts the foot in a better condition to follow the swiftness of the wrist, in most of the actions of the sword; nor can any thing contribute more to the equal situation, and to the retention of the body, qualities, which keeping you covered from the time of your combatant, procures you the means, not only of taking advantage of his, but also of possessing firmness, freedom, justness and swiftness. You are to observe two sorts of beating, the one with the foot firm in the same place, the other gaining measure; the beat with the foot firm, is done in two ways, the one in *appels*, or *alurements* on the blade, and the other in engagements or feints. That upon the *allurement* on the blade, may be made by a single beat of the foot, but those who are pretty well advanced, make two without lifting the foot but once, the first with the point, and the other with the whole foot: that on engagements or single feints, should have but one beat, the thrust being to be made on the second motion. The beat of the foot in marching or advancing, is also divided into two sorts, the one in engagements or single feints, and the other in engagements and feints following, or in double feints; the manner of engaging must be with a single beat gaining measure, and that of engaging with a double feint, must be done with a double beat, in order to agree with the motion of the wrist; and as in all, including the lunge, there must be three beats; you must, on the first time or feint, beat with the whole foot in the same place, at the second motion of the wrist beat again with the foot getting measure, and at the third motion push.

You must observe, that between the first and second motion, there is no interval, but between the second and third there is, in order to see where the enemy gives light: this interval must be shorter or longer according as your disposition or practice is more or less.

CHAPTER 25
Of the Good Effects of a Nice Discernment of the Eye

In fencing, there is the foreseen, and the unforeseen; the foreseen is the effect of the understanding and of the will, and the unforeseen is the effect of the discernment of the eye, and of custom; which being upheld by this quality, has no sooner discerned an action or opening of the enemy, than all the parts which are to act, display themselves to oppose or attack him, as if they depended on the eye. To be convinced of this truth, you may reflect on *reading*, wherein, as soon as the eye has discerned the words, the pronouncing them follows as quick as in a studied discourse; the eye and tongue being so disposed by custom, as to do it without immediately reflecting. Indeed before they could arrive to this, the understanding and the will were necessary, which having been united for a certain time, have communicated such a habit to these parts, as to make them act as it were of themselves.

In order to acquire this quality in fencing, it is necessary that the master, in his lessons, should show what opportunities are to be favourably laid hold of, two opposite actions at one and the same time, that whilst he is uncovering some part of his body, he cannot, at the same instant, parry, because by the parade, it must be covered; so that by making them make their thrusts, and other motions, by the discernment of the eye, they find themselves by practice ready to oppose all the motions of the antagonist without the assistance of the will. This method is indeed a little more tedious in the beginning, but it afterwards becomes shorter and more certain.

If you have not had practice enough to make the discernment of the eye thus habitual, you must observe what motions your action causes in the adversary, by making a half, or home-thrust, in order to discover whether the enemy has recourse to the parade, or to the time: if he goes to parry, you must observe his manner, in order to make a feint resembling the same thrust, and to push at the part where you observed him to give the light; and if he goes to the time, you also make a feint, preparing yourself for the parade and riposte, or to take a time contrary to his.

CHAPTER 26
Of Time

If we were to follow the exact term of time, every thing that is done in fencing might be called so; for you should never thrust but when you have a favourable opportunity of hitting, nor parry, but at the time that favours you to oppose the enemy's sword, not make an engagement, nor a feint, but to take the time upon the motion that your action occasions in the adversary.

Time is the duration of any motion: it is called time because it is the most favourable opportunity of pushing, the enemy being unable during one action to do a contrary one.

It is divided into several manners and terms: the first is called the time, the second, taking his time, the third, time to time, the fourth, the same time, and the fifth, false time.

1. Taking the time, is making your thrust by a judicious discernment on the motion of the enemy, taking him by a contrary one: you are to know that every motion, of whatever part it be, is called time; for which reason, I shall say nothing of feints, engagements, and disengagements, upon which it may be taken; and that in three manners, *viz.* straight, lowering the body, or *volting* it, which you must know how to apply. In a straight thrust the time should be taken by lowering and *volting* the body, because the thrust coming straight, if you were to push the same way, you would, by supporting the wrist, make a *contrast*; and by pushing crooked, you would make a *coup fourres*, or an interchanged thrust; but if the thrust be in two times, or motions, you may push on the first; if it be in three motions, on the second. as to the *volting* and lowering the body, they may be used on all motions, provided

they be abandoned, and that the enemy does not keep back his body to draw you on.

2. Taking his time, is the most subtle thing in fencing, depending principally on the mind: the manner of taking it proceeds from your place or situation, which gives you an opportunity of knowing the *fort* and the *feeble* of the enemy, so that feeling his blade with yours, you may by a judicious custom, push at a proper instant, according as you find the weakness of his sword; and though it may seem that the enemy, in the same guard, and at the same distance, can as easily parry; that does not happen because of his different design to push, disengage, or make a feint, by reason of the several operations of the mind which follow the will.

3. The time to time, or the counter to time, is by several people, called counter-time: this cannot in effect alter this necessary part of the art; it being but an impropriety in terms; when they say that making a motion to bring the enemy on, and when he is going to make a thrust, the making a counter; this is by consequence a counter time, like a counter-disengagement, without observing that a counter-time is nothing but an ill timed motion, which should upon all occasions be avoided: and if that argument were to take place, it might be said that there is no such thing in fencing as taking the time, because it is to be done only by taking a time contrary to that which is intended to be taken of you, which according to their argument would be a counter-time; whereas the term time to time, or counter to time, sufficiently shows, that it requires three motions; since the taking the time requires two, and the taking it at the time that he takes it, must require a third. Of these three motions you are to make two: the first, in order to get one from the enemy, that you may have an advantage by your second, which is the third time; so that when he thinks to take the time upon you, you take it upon him, which, far from being a counter-time, is a time to his, or counter to his time.

4. The same time, depends on three things: first, that both having a design to push, you both push by chance at once, without expecting it from each other: secondly: that full of the design to take the time, and not knowing it, you push upon the enemy's thrust, without foreseeing how to avoid it; and thirdly, when an

inferior or desperate man, unable to defend himself, had rather run on your thrust in endeavouring to hit you, than strive in vain to avoid it. these are not only the occasions of the same time, but also of the *coups fourres*.

It is to be observed, that time, and the same time, differ only in their figure, and not in their occasion, as Monsieur De la Touche says, for to take the time upon a thrust, you must go off upon the lunge, as if it were on the same time, except that the figure of the body shuns the thrust, which in that of the same time it does not do.

5. false time, is a motion made by the enemy to draw you on, in order to take a time upon yours; therefore he that would take the time, should distinguish whether the motion made, is to disorder him, and take the advantage of his parade, or to make him thrust, and take the advantage of his lunge; in case of the first, it would be a fault not to push; and in case of the other, it would be amiss to push. some masters call the false time, half time, which is wrong, every motion being a time, and as it is impossible to make a half motion, so it is impossible to make a half time.

The difference of time between the dexterous and awkward is, that the dexterous present and take the time, and the others, give and lose it.

CHAPTER 27
Of Swiftness

Swiftness is the shortness of time between the beginning and end of a motion: it proceeds from a regular and frequent exercise, joined with a good disposition; that is to say, vigour and suppleness, which form agility.

A great swiftness cannot be acquired without long practice and a good disposition, the one not being sufficient, without the other, to give it: for the best natural parts, without practice, will be of very little service to those who have the best disposition; and the most regular practice without the assistance of nature, will never make a man perfectly swift.

Swiftness in fencing, is so necessary, that without this quality, it is very difficult to defend, and impossible to offend: this truth is so well known, that every one is earnestly desirous of it, though most people are ignorant of the means necessary to acquire it.

What contributes most to the becoming swift, besides, frequent exercise and a fine disposition, is a perfect situation of the parts, the retention of the body, and the regular motion of the wrist: the situation requires this advantageous point of all the parts, to communicate freedom and vigour to the action, that they may act with quickness. In order to retain the body, it is necessary that it be always in it's perfect situation, during the motions previous to the thrust; and if the thrust consist of one time only, the wrist must begin.

As to the motion of the hand, it must not only be animated, but also the action must not be wide, whether in disengagements, engagements, feints, or ripostes; because if you would be soon at your mark, it is not sufficient to go quick, but it is also necessary that the action be close.

Many people have confounded the swiftness of pushing with precipitate or consecutive thrusts, without considering that precipitation is either when the body moves before the hand, or when an improper motion is made; and the consecutive thrusts, the pushing several times without interval, or when there is no occasion; which may be done by one who is not swift; for swiftness is only the shortness of time between the beginning and end of an action, as I have already said.

Swiftness and time are very justly called the soul of fencing, and all thrusts owe their success to these qualities; for you cannot hit but by surprise, nor surprise but by swiftness.

There are three ways of surprising in fencing: the first is the situation of the guard, taking his time: the second, is doing an action to disorder the enemy, in order to hit him, at that time, where he is open; and the third is when the opponent attacks you, either by feints, engagements, or lunges, you take him upon the time. though these three sorts of surprise require a certain point of swiftness, the first needs the most, having no other support; but the two others have the advantage of having disordered the enemy.

Although time, swiftness, and the other qualities are absolutely necessary in fencing, without their just concurrence they are useless. In order to acquire which, the wrist must be easy by practice, that you may hit where you see light.

CHAPTER 28
Of Measure

Time, swiftness, and justness, without the knowledge of measure, would be in vain, thrusts from afar being of no use, and from near, dangerous; and the other motions should also be at a certain distance, in order not only to be ready for the time, but also to take advantage of the disorder of the enemy. The measure is taken from you to the enemy, and from the enemy to you: the first is easier known, as well because it is naturally so, as by the custom of your lunge, which being, in regard of yourself, always the same, makes it easier by practice: the measure from the enemy to you is difficult, from the difference in persons whose stature, activity, or swords, are not always alike; and though the height should be the same, the arms, thighs and legs are not proportionable; besides there are big men that have short arms, and little men that have long arms. It is likewise so in regard to the cleft; some being longer in the fork than others; and though two men should in that particular be alike, if one of them has shorter legs than the other, he will reach farther, because his thighs are longer, and in the lunge, only one of the legs contributes to it's length, the other making a line almost perpendicular, whereas the two thighs making a straight line, contribute equally to the extension.

The difference in suppleness, also makes a difference in the extension; a man who has the freedom of his shoulders and hips, going farther than one that has them constrained. It may also happen that two men of like proportion and freedom of parts, may not have an equal extension, by their being taught differently; some masters teaching to keep the body upright, the wrist raised, or too much on one side, and the left-foot first; whereas the body should lean a little forward, without raising or carrying the hand to one side, farther than to keep the body covered, and the left-foot should lie down on the edge; this situation gives a greater length than the other.

The different lengths of swords sometimes make it difficult to know the measure, and makes it impossible to fix it by rule, as several masters have pretended: some of them say that the measure is just, when the points cross each other a foot; others, with as little reason, would have the middle of your blade touch the point of the adversary's; but what gives a true knowledge of the measure is frequent exercise, accompanied with a good judgment, pushing often *quart* and *tierce* with different foils, and being pushed at by different persons.

The extension is taken from the left-foot, which is the centre, to the button of the foil.

I did design, in this place, to treat of time, and of a regular way of pushing in lessons, from the beginning to the end of one year, according to the disposition of scholars; but after I had finished it, I thought that my fellow-brethren would perhaps take it ill that I should prescribe lessons to their scholars, by which, instead of gaining their good opinion, I might incur the accusation of being more busy than knowing.

CHAPTER 29
Of the Necessity of Some Qualities in a Master

In order to teach well, it's necessary to have a perfect idea of the means which conduce from the beginning to the end of the matter proposed, I mean to it's perfection, or to what comes nearest it, if our age has not as yet arrived to it.

In fencing, as well as in other exercises, there should be judgment and knowledge how to act and how to teach: the first is the effect of a long and good theory; the second, of a good theory, long practice, and a good disposition; and the third, besides the theory and practice, is the effect of a good genius, or of a particular talent.

Qualities which should be always united; so that the genius may be capable of teaching properly to different persons, the application of the rules which are acquired by experience.

It is as necessary in this art that a master's motions should be regular, and that he should hold the foil properly in his hand, as it is for a writing master to draw the example well that he would have copied; so that the scholar of the one, or of the other, may learn a better motion, or a finer character. It is also proper that when a scholar commits a fault, the master should shame him by imitating it, the seeing the fault making a greater impression than the hearing of it.

A master in his lesson should give a time to the scholar to make him push, in order to teach him to take the enemy's time. He should likewise sometimes beat back his body, and parry him from time to time, that he may accustom him to be firm on his legs, to oppose his sword well, and to recover well: it is good sometimes to let him make several thrusts following, and then remaining firm all of a sudden, to show him, that he should always be ready to thrust when an opportunity offers, and to retain himself when it does not offer.

In order to make him take the time well, and to form his parade and riposte properly, the time that the master gives must have a regard to rule, and sometimes to the disorder of an unskilful enemy, that he may be equally fortified for both; and to form his parade and riposte the master must push in the manner the most like to an assault.

Though most masters give lessons with shorter and stiffer foils than are used in assaulting or playing loose, I esteem it better always to use the same foils that they may not be deceived in an assault.

A master's play should be neat, subtle agreeable, and useful, as fit for combat as for the school.

The art of fencing being to make the most of a good or bad disposition, when it is good it is capable of being made perfectly dexterous, and when bad, the defect of nature is to be repaired by art.

By saying that it is no hard matter to perfect such men as are naturally of a very good disposition, is meant the bringing them to a certain point which they could almost arrive to of themselves, by practice and speculation; but it is well known that it is the business of a good master to make his scholar perfectly dexterous, and though he may have a good disposition and long exercise, if he is not well instructed, he cannot become dexterous, even though he should execute with agility, being incapable of acquiring a good without knowing and practising it.

A good disposition is seldom to be met with, for there is generally a mixture of bad parts with the good. Some have a supple, light and vigorous body, and with these qualities a heavy or ill adjusted hand; and others that have as good a disposition as is desirable, have a narrow genius, fearing to undertake any thing, or are hot and inconsiderate, which shows that it is only be a perfect accord of the parts and understanding that a man can be perfectly dexterous.

In short an able master does not only show the fault, and whence it proceeds, but also the danger to which it exposes, and the means to leave it. A master whose play is regular, or who has the best foundation, may properly be said to be a good master.

CHAPTER 30

Rules for Pushing and Parrying at the Wall, and for Making an Assault

Though it is absolutely necessary to begin by way of lesson, and to continue in it a long time, in order that practice growing to a habit, may give liberty to the parts to form themselves: nevertheless however well you may take your lessons, some other means are necessary to make an assault well, than those which the master gives at his *plastron*: this rule must be supported by pushing and parrying at the wall, and in the manner I am going to lay down.

When you have laboured a certain time at lessons, you must push at a cushion which is fixed against the wall for that purpose, observing the guard, and the measure or extension of the thrust; and that the hand display itself in *quart*, not only according to the rule, but first, adjusting and supporting the thrust, and that all the parts be placed in the most advantageous situation for the thrust and recovery, which should be very regularly observed.

After having lunged for some days on the cushion, to fix the wrist and body a little, you must push at a scholar, who being placed at the wall will parry your thrusts; you should be in measure, and to see if it be just, you must lunge in *quart*, placing the button softly on the body, at the same time taking off your hat, having taken the measure you must recover in guard, and place yourself on the outside of his sword in order to disengage and push *quart*, being more careful of pushing justly than hitting; he that parries should from time to time drop his foil, which will show whether he that pushes follows the blade or the line of the body; having remained some time upon the lunge to form the support of the wrist and the posture of the body you recover to guard. When you lunge pretty well in *quart*, you may disengage and push *tierce*, and when the thrust is pushed and parried, you may recover and push *seconde* under.

When you have pushed for some time in this manner, you may practise to parry, putting yourself for that purpose to the wall, which furnishes a better parade than at large, where you are used to draw back the body which weakens it, whereas here you cannot, which makes the parade stronger, having no dependence but on the foil; you should choose a scholar that pushes the most regularly, it being difficult without that, that a beginner should learn to parry justly.

Most young beginners endeavour to hit at any rate, instead of practising what would be beneficial to them, but instead of deceiving others they deceive themselves, by practising less how to form themselves and push according to rule, than how to spoil their bodies, and destroy the solidity of the principles: some use themselves to push with the wrist only, without the foot, which is dangerous, by reason of the too great measure; others with as little reason, and as much danger, place themselves without binding the blade, and thrust under the wrist; in the one the situation of the guard is good for nothing, and in the other there is no defence if the adversary thrusts at that time: others deceive by making a time or motion when they are placed, but the pushing at the wall requires only the justness and swiftness of the thrust; others put themselves very near baulking the measure, which may be done four ways, though the left-foot may be in it's proper place, and kept firm in the thrust; the first is done by marking or bringing forward the point of the left-foot, keeping it a little in, then advancing the heel, which gives more measure; secondly, by keeping back the body on a lunge, you deceive the measure and hit by abandoning it forward, which gives it a greater extension, thirdly, by raising or carrying the wrist too high, or too much to one side, which shortening the thrust, makes it believed that you are out of reach, but according to the rule and line you are too much in reach; fourthly, some take measure by holding the thumb on the body of the guard, and when they have a mind to hit they hold it on the middle of the handle, with the pommel in the hand, which also gives a greater length.

When you have for some time used yourself to push and parry

at the wall, according to the rules that I have laid down, you must, (though it is not the rule of schools, especially when you push with strangers,) you must I say, when you push with a scholar of your own master, push and parry a thrust alternately, disengaging, and then do the same feinting, and sometime after you should make the other thrusts, telling one another your design, which makes you execute and parry them by rule, especially if you reflect on the motions and postures of the lunges and parades. Being a little formed to this method, you may, being warned of the thrust, parry it, telling the adversary where you intend your riposte, which puts him in a condition to avoid it, and gives him room to redouble after his parade, either straight or by a feint, at which you are not surprised, expecting by being forewarned the thrust he is to make, which puts you easily on your defence and offence: by this manner of exercise, you may not only improve faster, but with more art, the eye and parts being insensibly disposed to follow the rule, whereas without this method, the difference that there is between a lesson of assaulting a man who forewarns you, helps you, and lets you hit him, and another who endeavours to defend himself and hit you, is, that except the practice of lessons be very well taught by long exercise, you fall into a disorder which is often owing to the want of art more than to any defect in nature. The taking a lesson well, and the manner of pushing and parrying which I have just described, may be attained to by practice only, but some other things are necessary to make an assault well; for besides the turn of the body, the lightness, suppleness and vigour which compose the exterior part, you must be stout and prudent, qualities so essential, that without them you cannot act with a good grace, nor to the purpose. If you are apprehensive, besides, that you don't push home, or justly, fear making you keep back your thrust, or follow the blade, the least motion of the enemy disorders you, and puts you out of a condition to hit him, and to avoid his thrusts. Without prudence, you cannot take the advantage of the situation, motions designs of the enemy, which changing very often, according to his capacity and to the measure, demonstrates that an ill concerted enterprise exposes more to danger than it procures advantage: in order to turn this quality to an advantage, you are to observe the enemy's *fort* and *feeble*, whether he attack or defend; if he attack it will be either by plain thrusts straight, or disengaged, or by feints or engagements, which may be opposed by time, or ripostes: if he keeps on his defence, it is either to take the time or to riposte. In case of the first; you should, by half thrusts, oblige him to push in order to take a counter to his time, and if he sticks to his parade you must serve in what manner, in order to disorder him by feints, and push where he gives light.

It would fill a whole volume to describe the thrusts that may be made, according to the difference of persons, as well to surprise as to avoid being surprised; besides the many repetitions would be extremely puzzling, for which reason, I have, instead of them, laid down the following advices, which contain chiefly, what I could not otherwise have communicated without a long treatise.

Don't put yourself in guard within the reach of the enemy.

Make no wry faces, or motions that are disagreeable to the sight.

Be not affected, negligent, nor stiff.

Don't flatter yourself in your lessons, and still less in assaults.

Be not angry at receiving a thrust, but take care to avoid it.

Be not vain at the thrusts you give, nor show contempt when you receive them.

Do not endeavour to give many thrusts, running the risk of receiving one.

Don't think yourself expert, but that you may become so.

When you present the foils, give the choice without pressing.

If you are much inferior, make no long assaults.

Do nothing that's useless, every action should tend to your advantage.

Lessons and assaults are only valuable when the application and genius make them so.

Too good an opinion spoils many people, and too bad a one still more.

A natural Disposition and Practice are necessary in Lessons, but in Assaults there must be a Genius besides.

The goodness of lessons and of assaults does not consist so much in the length as in the manner of them.

When you have to do with one that's bold and forward, it is necessary to seem apprehensive in order to get a favourable opportunity.

If you act against one that's fearful, attack him briskly to put him in disorder.

Before you applaud a thrust given, examine if chance had no hand in it.

Thrusts of experience, and those of chance are different, the first come often, the others seldom or never happen, you may depend on one, but not on the other.

In battle let valour and prudence go together, the lion's courage with the fox's craft.

To be in possession of what you know, you must be in possession of yourself.

Undertake nothing but what your strength and the capacity of the enemy will admit of in the execution.

The beauty of an assault appears in the execution of the design.

Make no thrust without considering the advantage and the danger of it.

If the eye and wrist precede the body, the execution will be good.

Be always cautious, time lost cannot be regained.

If you can hit without a feint, make none, two motions are more dangerous than one.

To know what you risk, you must know what you are worth.

If you would do well, acquire the agreeable and useful.

Twenty good qualities will not make you perfect, and one bad one will hinder your being so.

Judge of a thrust, rather by reason than by it's success; the one may fail, but the other cannot.

To parry well is much, but it is nothing when you can do more.

Let your guard, and your play be always directly opposite to the enemy.

Practice is either a good or an evil; all consists in the choice of it.

When you think yourself skilful and dexterous, it is then you are not so.

It is not enough that your parts agree, they must also answer the enemy's motions.

The knowing a good without practising it, turns to an evil.

Two skilful men acting together, fight more with their heads than with their hands.

If you are superior to your enemy, press him close, and if you are inferior, break measure to keep him moving.

Endeavour both to discover the enemy's design, and to conceal your own.

When the eye and the hand agree in the same instant, you are perfectly right.

Draw not your sword, but to serve the king, preserve your honour, or defend your Life.

CHAPTER 31
Against Several Erroneous Opinions

Though there are people of a bad taste in every art or science, there are more in that of fencing than in others, as well by reason of the little understanding of some teachers, as of the little practice of some learners, who are not acting upon a good foundation, or long enough, to have a good idea of it, argue so weakly on this exercise, that I thought it as much my business to observe their errors, as it is my duty to instruct those that I have the honour to teach in the theory of it: by this means, I may furnish the one with juster sentiments, and the others with the means of preserving their honour and lives.

I begin with those, who defer letting their children learn until they have attained a certain age, growth and strength. If these three qualities would enable them to put this art in execution immediately, I acknowledge that they ought not to begin until they possessed them; but it is by long experience and practice only, that they can become perfect; so that except they begin young, the employments for which they are designed, may not give them time to arrive to it; besides, by beginning in a tender age, the body is more easily brought to a good air, and an easy disengagement; being more at liberty, and less used to faults, which it would naturally fall into for want of being cultivated.

Others say that it is needless to learn when the disposition is wanting, which is an error; for a body that is well disposed by nature, can better dispense with the want of improvement, than those that she has taken less care of; these requiring a constant labour, to acquire what the others have almost of themselves; and though they cannot arrive to a perfect agility, yet their bodies will be better disposed to act, and their lives not so much in danger.

Some assure you that the knowing how to fence, makes a man quarrelsome, and thereby exposes him to dangerous consequences, without considering it is a natural brutality, honour, or danger, which obliges him to attack another, or defend himself, which he would do without having learned, with this difference; that though he have the same brutality or courage, the issue of the battle is not the same; and if he have occasion to defend himself, would it not be better for him to be able to do it, than to leave his life to an uncertain and dangerous hazard.

Others say that it is enough to learn one exercise at a time; that a plurality of different lessons fatigues the mind and the body: but as one science disposes the mind for the others, they having a sort of a correspondence one with another, so exercises favour one another as well in regard to the posture of the body, as to the freedom of motion; besides, that learning them one after another, as each particular would take up as much time as all in general, this length of time would be too great for any one almost to succeed in them.

Many people say that with sword in hand the rules of the school are not observed, and that it is sufficient to have a good heart: it is certain that people who are subject to this error, are not capable of following the rules which are to be acquired only by putting a good theory in practice; which by frequent use, disposes the eye and the part of executing so well, that it is almost impossible to act otherwise: and as to the practice of schools and of the sword, it is the same; for no one ought to do any thing with the foil, but what he knows by experience to be without risk, according to his rules. In some cases, it is true, what is esteemed good in one, is not in the other. For example: thrusts with the foil are good only on the body, and with the sword they are good every where; and that in an assault with the foil, the joining is reckoned as nothing, whereas in battle it is the seal of the victory; but except in that, it should be alike in every thing.

Others say that if they had to do with experienced men, they would not give them time to put themselves in guard; as if a man who is expert were not always on his guard, being more knowing, and better disposed, not only to place himself at once, by the habit that all his parts have contrasted, but also to surprise, and to avoid being surprised, by the knowledge he has of time and measure: on the contrary, an unskilful person being ignorant of both, is easily caught; besides, that his parts being unaccustomed to place themselves regularly, or at once, must always be in a continual motion, vainly seeking their place, by which they give the time, and would lose it if it were given to them.

Some, in opposition to these, say that if they know how to keep themselves in guard it is sufficient. They are in the right if the guard be perfect, which is not to be acquired but by a practice as long as is necessary to make them perfectly dexterous, which is not their meaning; they thinking that it is only the placing of the parts, which is useless, without freedom and vigour to manage them. These are qualities which when accompanied with a certain regular air, and a good grace, show, as soon as a man takes a sword or foil in his hand, to what pitch of dexterity he is arrived.

Some men will tell you that they know enough to serve their turn: those who use this expression, as well as those I have spoken of before, sufficiently show that they have learnt but little or nothing. In effect it is no hard matter to judge of the different degrees of ability; so that when a man finds himself inferior, he cannot properly say that he knows enough to serve his turn; and a man who is superior, knows very well that he is not perfect, and that if his good disposition together with his long practice, has brought him very forward in the art, others may know as much as he, and that therefore he is not so perfect as an unskilful person may imagine.

I have heard several people say that they did not care to be dexterous, nor to know the five rules, provided they knew how to defend themselves, and to push and parry well; and really they are in the right, supposing they could do that without practising what the most able men have invented upon this occasion.

There are people that say, that with sword in hand, against an able man, there is nothing to be done but push vigorously, to disorder him: I am apt to believe that this may succeed against a man who is not well formed, or has not the courage and resolution that is necessary; but if he has enough to keep up his spirit, this attack will be advantageous to him; because it cannot be done without giving him an opportunity of getting the better; and besides, I have reason to believe that the greatest part of those who talk in this manner, would hardly attempt an able man.

It may be said that people have then fought in this manner with success; but as there is difference in persons, what succeeded with them against unskilful people or cowards, would have been dangerous against other men.

I have met with people who were weak enough to believe that knowledge in fencing takes away the heart, saying, that seeing the counters to every thrust they form, by means of that knowledge, an idea of evident danger, which dissipating the courage, and causing an apprehension, hinders them from their enterprise; when an unskilful person blindly undertakes every thing. It is true that there is great blindness in this way of pushing, as they say, and still more in their understanding, to think that an able man dares not undertake or venture when the appearance of success leads him to it; and that an ignorant man shall venture when his loss is almost certain. Is it reasonable to suppose, that a man of natural courage should lose it, because he is assured that he is more expert than his enemy, over whom, or perhaps his equals, he always had the better in assaults, by the help of his knowledge and dexterity? This, far from intimidating him, seems to assure him of success, which is due to his habitual practice. On the contrary, an awkward man having seen, by his disadvantage in school assaults, that he has no room to hope in combat, the dexterous man possessing the qualities which procure success, and one who had never handled a foil, will be as much puzzled, as if he had experienced the disadvantage of it.

Others, with as little reason, leave all to chance, but the very name is sufficient to show that it is not to be relied on.

Some again say to what purpose shall we learn to fence, the king had forbid duels: it is true that this great prince, as august for his piety as for his victories, was willing thereby to preserve the blood of his bravest subjects, who exposed it every day to be shed through a false notion of honour.

But though he forbid duels, he was so far from hindering the practice of the sword, that he has established several academies for the perfect use of it, not only for defence, but also to qualify his subjects to put the justice of his measures in execution: and it must at last be agreed to, that a man who wears a sword, without knowing how to use it, runs as great a hazard, and is full as ridiculous, as a man who carries books about him without knowing how to read.

Many men are of opinion that a man may naturally know enough to attack or defend himself, without the assistance of art: man, though the only reasonable creature, finds himself deprived of what irrational creatures naturally possess; and he requires for his improvement the assistance and practice of others; the grand art of war, and that of using the sword, which has been practised through so many ages, still find new inventions; and it may be said, that as there is no place, in whatever situation by nature, but requires art to secure it's defence; so likewise, whatever disposition a man possesses, he cannot be perfect without the assistance of rules and practice.

Some men acknowledge that skill is necessary in single combat, but that in a crowd or battle it is altogether useless: I own that on these occasions, it is less useful than in single battle, by reason of the different accidents, as of cannon, muskets, and of other arms; besides, a man may be attacked by several at once: but if a man cannot avoid being hit with a ball, and sometimes with a sword, he may, nevertheless, by the disposition and agility of the parts, more easily defend and return a thrust: besides, being more able to hit with the edge or point, he may put more enemies to flight, or keep them at a greater distance. If the French troops have always been victorious, sword in hand, a part of the glory is owing to the skill of several officers; and I'll venture to say, that if they had all been as expert as they should have been, you might see, as well on foot as on horseback, in battle as on a breach, actions that would be not only uncommon but prodigious. It may perhaps be said, that our enemies have some expert officers among them; besides, that their number is commonly less than in France, there is as great a difference between their dexterity and that of the French, as between their masters and ours, from whom very few would have learned if the war had no suspended our academies.[1]

I think it proper to finish this chapter by confuting an error as common, and more ridiculous, than the others; which is, of an infallible thrust, which a great many people think that masters reserve for dangerous occasions, or to sell it at a dear rate. This wonderful

---

1. As in this Paragraph, Monsieur L'Abbat rather introduces an encomium on his countrymen, than any thing essential to the art of fencing. I leave the reader to his own opinion thereon.

thing, is called the secret thrust. I don't know whether this error proceeded from those who have not learned, or from the chimera of some self-conceited masters, who have sold to ignorant scholars, some thrusts as infallible, of their own contrivance, as ridiculous and dangerous as the simplicity of the scholar and the knavery of the master are great.

To discover the error of this opinion you must observe two things: first, that in fencing there are no more than five thrusts or places, which I have described earlier, showing the parade of each of them; and secondly, that there is no motion without it's opposite; so that as you cannot push without a motion, there is no thrust without it's counter, and even several; for besides the different positions of the body, there is not only the time to take, but also several parades to favour the ripostes, which plainly shows, that doing one of these things properly, this imaginary infallible thrust, far from succeeding will expose him that would make it.

All the secrets in the thrusts that are given by an able man, far from being an effect of the thrust, is only an effect of the occasion, and the swiftness; or rather of the judgment and practice: by means of these qualities all thrusts are secret ones, or they would be worth nothing.

All the thrusts in fencing are equally good, when they are made according to rule, with swiftness, and on the occasions proper to them; wherefore they ought not to be neglected whilst the time of learning them offers; not but you may stick closer to some thrusts than to others, either because you may be better disposed for them, or because you are more used to them.

I thought that after I had exposed the errors of several persons, I might tell them, that it is contrary to the rules of good breeding, to talk of things they do not understand; that oftentimes people, by their first appearance, have been thought to possess the qualities of knowing men, but have afterwards forfeited the good opinion which they had at first imposed on others.

Thrusts of Emulation for Prizes, Wagers &c.

All thrusts from the neckband to the waistband are counted good.

Coup fourres or interchanged thrusts are not counted on either side, except one of the competitors has recourse to it in order to make the thrusts equal, then the thrust of the other is good, and not his.

If one hits the body and the other the face or below the waist at the same time; the thrust on the body is counted, but not the other.

If a man parries with his hand, and afterwards hit, his thrust is not good, because by parrying with the hand, his antagonist's foil is less at liberty than if he had parried with the blade, and might be a reason why he could not parry and riposte.

If a man takes the time, opposing with the left-hand, and hits without receiving, his thrust is not good, because if he had not opposed with the hand, both would have hit, the opposition of the hand serving only to avoid, but no way contributing to the success of the thrust.

If in parrying, binding, or lashing the foil, it falls, and that the thrust is made without interval, it is good.

Thrusts made with the sword in both hands, or shifting from one hand to the other are not good.

A master is not to give judgment for his own scholar.

LEONAUR

ALSO FROM LEONAUR

AVAILABLE IN SOFTCOVER OR HARDCOVER WITH DUST JACKET

THE 2ND MAORI WAR: 1860-1861 *by Robert Carey*—The Second Maori War, or First Taranaki War, one more bloody instalment of the conflicts between European settlers and the indigenous Maori people.

A JOURNAL OF THE SECOND SIKH WAR *by Daniel A. Sandford*—The Experiences of an Ensign of the 2nd Bengal European Regiment During the Campaign in the Punjab, India, 1848-49.

THE LIGHT INFANTRY OFFICER *by John H. Cooke*—The Experiences of an Officer of the 43rd Light Infantry in America During the War of 1812.

BUSHVELDT CARBINEERS *by George Witton*—The War Against the Boers in South Africa and the 'Breaker' Morant Incident.

LAKE'S CAMPAIGNS IN INDIA *by Hugh Pearse*—The Second Anglo Maratha War, 1803-1807.

BRITAIN IN AFGHANISTAN 1: THE FIRST AFGHAN WAR 1839-42 *by Archibald Forbes*—From invasion to destruction-a British military disaster.

BRITAIN IN AFGHANISTAN 2: THE SECOND AFGHAN WAR 1878-80 *by Archibald Forbes*—This is the history of the Second Afghan War-another episode of British military history typified by savagery, massacre, siege and battles.

UP AMONG THE PANDIES *by Vivian Dering Majendie*—Experiences of a British Officer on Campaign During the Indian Mutiny, 1857-1858.

MUTINY: 1857 *by James Humphries*—Authentic Voices from the Indian Mutiny-First Hand Accounts of Battles, Sieges and Personal Hardships.

BLOW THE BUGLE, DRAW THE SWORD *by W. H. G. Kingston*—The Wars, Campaigns, Regiments and Soldiers of the British & Indian Armies During the Victorian Era, 1839-1898.

WAR BEYOND THE DRAGON PAGODA *by Major J. J. Snodgrass*—A Personal Narrative of the First Anglo-Burmese War 1824 - 1826.

THE HERO OF ALIWAL *by James Humphries*—The Campaigns of Sir Harry Smith in India, 1843-1846, During the Gwalior War & the First Sikh War.

ALL FOR A SHILLING A DAY *by Donald F. Featherstone*—The story of H.M. 16th, the Queen's Lancers During the first Sikh War 1845-1846.

LEONAUR

ALSO FROM LEONAUR
AVAILABLE IN SOFTCOVER OR HARDCOVER WITH DUST JACKET

AT THEM WITH THE BAYONET *by Donald F. Featherstone*—The first Anglo-Sikh War 1845-1846.

STEPHEN CRANE'S BATTLES *by Stephen Crane*—Nine Decisive Battles Recounted by the Author of 'The Red Badge of Courage'.

THE GURKHA WAR *by H. T. Prinsep*—The Anglo-Nepalese Conflict in North East India 1814-1816.

FIRE & BLOOD *by G. R. Gleig*—The burning of Washington & the battle of New Orleans, 1814, through the eyes of a young British soldier.

SOUND ADVANCE! *by Joseph Anderson*—Experiences of an officer of HM 50th regiment in Australia, Burma & the Gwalior war.

THE CAMPAIGN OF THE INDUS *by Thomas Holdsworth*—Experiences of a British Officer of the 2nd (Queen's Royal) Regiment in the Campaign to Place Shah Shuja on the Throne of Afghanistan 1838 - 1840.

WITH THE MADRAS EUROPEAN REGIMENT IN BURMA *by John Butler*—The Experiences of an Officer of the Honourable East India Company's Army During the First Anglo-Burmese War 1824 - 1826.

IN ZULULAND WITH THE BRITISH ARMY *by Charles L. Norris-Newman*—The Anglo-Zulu war of 1879 through the first-hand experiences of a special correspondent.

BESIEGED IN LUCKNOW *by Martin Richard Gubbins*—The first Anglo-Sikh War 1845-1846.

A TIGER ON HORSEBACK *by L. March Phillips*—The Experiences of a Trooper & Officer of Rimington's Guides - The Tigers - during the Anglo-Boer war 1899 - 1902.

SEPOYS, SIEGE & STORM *by Charles John Griffiths*—The Experiences of a young officer of H.M.'s 61st Regiment at Ferozepore, Delhi ridge and at the fall of Delhi during the Indian mutiny 1857.

CAMPAIGNING IN ZULULAND *by W. E. Montague*—Experiences on campaign during the Zulu war of 1879 with the 94th Regiment.

THE STORY OF THE GUIDES *by G.J. Younghusband*—The Exploits of the Soldiers of the famous Indian Army Regiment from the northwest frontier 1847 - 1900.

LEONAUR

ALSO FROM LEONAUR
AVAILABLE IN SOFTCOVER OR HARDCOVER WITH DUST JACKET

ZULU:1879 *by D.C.F. Moodie & the Leonaur Editors*—The Anglo-Zulu War of 1879 from contemporary sources: First Hand Accounts, Interviews, Dispatches, Official Documents & Newspaper Reports.

THE RED DRAGOON *by W.J. Adams*—With the 7th Dragoon Guards in the Cape of Good Hope against the Boers & the Kaffir tribes during the 'war of the axe' 1843-48'.

THE RECOLLECTIONS OF SKINNER OF SKINNER'S HORSE *by James Skinner*—James Skinner and his 'Yellow Boys' Irregular cavalry in the wars of India between the British, Mahratta, Rajput, Mogul, Sikh & Pindarree Forces.

A CAVALRY OFFICER DURING THE SEPOY REVOLT *by A. R. D. Mackenzie*—Experiences with the 3rd Bengal Light Cavalry, the Guides and Sikh Irregular Cavalry from the outbreak to Delhi and Lucknow.

A NORFOLK SOLDIER IN THE FIRST SIKH WAR *by J W Baldwin*—Experiences of a private of H.M. 9th Regiment of Foot in the battles for the Punjab, India 1845-6.

TOMMY ATKINS' WAR STORIES: 14 FIRST HAND ACCOUNTS—Fourteen first hand accounts from the ranks of the British Army during Queen Victoria's Empire.

THE WATERLOO LETTERS *by H. T. Siborne*—Accounts of the Battle by British Officers for its Foremost Historian.

NEY: GENERAL OF CAVALRY VOLUME 1—1769-1799 *by Antoine Bulos*—The Early Career of a Marshal of the First Empire.

NEY: MARSHAL OF FRANCE VOLUME 2—1799-1805 *by Antoine Bulos*—The Early Career of a Marshal of the First Empire.

AIDE-DE-CAMP TO NAPOLEON *by Philippe-Paul de Ségur*—For anyone interested in the Napoleonic Wars this book, written by one who was intimate with the strategies and machinations of the Emperor, will be essential reading.

TWILIGHT OF EMPIRE *by Sir Thomas Ussher & Sir George Cockburn*—Two accounts of Napoleon's Journeys in Exile to Elba and St. Helena: Narrative of Events by Sir Thomas Ussher & Napoleon's Last Voyage: Extract of a diary by Sir George Cockburn.

PRIVATE WHEELER *by William Wheeler*—The letters of a soldier of the 51st Light Infantry during the Peninsular War & at Waterloo.

LEONAUR

ALSO FROM LEONAUR
AVAILABLE IN SOFTCOVER OR HARDCOVER WITH DUST JACKET

CAPTAIN COIGNET *by Jean-Roch Coignet*—A Soldier of Napoleon's Imperial Guard from the Italian Campaign to Russia and Waterloo.

HUSSAR ROCCA *by Albert Jean Michel de Rocca*—A French cavalry officer's experiences of the Napoleonic Wars and his views on the Peninsular Campaigns against the Spanish, British And Guerilla Armies.

MARINES TO 95TH (RIFLES) *by Thomas Fernyhough*—The military experiences of Robert Fernyhough during the Napoleonic Wars.

LIGHT BOB *by Robert Blakeney*—The experiences of a young officer in H.M 28th & 36th regiments of the British Infantry during the Peninsular Campaign of the Napoleonic Wars 1804 - 1814.

WITH WELLINGTON'S LIGHT CAVALRY *by William Tomkinson*—The Experiences of an officer of the 16th Light Dragoons in the Peninsular and Waterloo campaigns of the Napoleonic Wars.

SERGEANT BOURGOGNE *by Adrien Bourgogne*—With Napoleon's Imperial Guard in the Russian Campaign and on the Retreat from Moscow 1812 - 13.

SURTEES OF THE 95TH (RIFLES) *by William Surtees*—A Soldier of the 95th (Rifles) in the Peninsular campaign of the Napoleonic Wars.

SWORDS OF HONOUR *by Henry Newbolt & Stanley L. Wood*—The Careers of Six Outstanding Officers from the Napoleonic Wars, the Wars for India and the American Civil War.

ENSIGN BELL IN THE PENINSULAR WAR *by George Bell*—The Experiences of a young British Soldier of the 34th Regiment 'The Cumberland Gentlemen' in the Napoleonic wars.

HUSSAR IN WINTER *by Alexander Gordon*—A British Cavalry Officer during the retreat to Corunna in the Peninsular campaign of the Napoleonic Wars.

THE COMPLEAT RIFLEMAN HARRIS *by Benjamin Harris as told to and transcribed by Captain Henry Curling, 52nd Regt. of Foot*—The adventures of a soldier of the 95th (Rifles) during the Peninsular Campaign of the Napoleonic Wars.

THE ADVENTURES OF A LIGHT DRAGOON *by George Farmer & G.R. Gleig*—A cavalryman during the Peninsular & Waterloo Campaigns, in captivity & at the siege of Bhurtpore, India.

LEONAUR

ALSO FROM LEONAUR
AVAILABLE IN SOFTCOVER OR HARDCOVER WITH DUST JACKET

THE RELUCTANT REBEL *by William G. Stevenson*—A young Kentuckian's experiences in the Confederate Infantry & Cavalry during the American Civil War..

BOOTS AND SADDLES *by Elizabeth B. Custer*—The experiences of General Custer's Wife on the Western Plains.

FANNIE BEERS' CIVIL WAR *by Fannie A. Beers*—A Confederate Lady's Experiences of Nursing During the Campaigns & Battles of the American Civil War.

LADY SALE'S AFGHANISTAN *by Florentia Sale*—An Indomitable Victorian Lady's Account of the Retreat from Kabul During the First Afghan War.

THE TWO WARS OF MRS DUBERLY *by Frances Isabella Duberly*—An Intrepid Victorian Lady's Experience of the Crimea and Indian Mutiny.

THE REBELLIOUS DUCHESS *by Paul F. S. Dermoncourt*—The Adventures of the Duchess of Berri and Her Attempt to Overthrow French Monarchy.

LADIES OF WATERLOO *by Charlotte A. Eaton, Magdalene de Lancey & Juana Smith*—The Experiences of Three Women During the Campaign of 1815: Waterloo Days by Charlotte A. Eaton, A Week at Waterloo by Magdalene de Lancey & Juana's Story by Juana Smith.

TWO YEARS BEFORE THE MAST *by Richard Henry Dana. Jr.*—The account of one young man's experiences serving on board a sailing brig—the Penelope—bound for California, between the years1834-36.

A SAILOR OF KING GEORGE *by Frederick Hoffman*—From Midshipman to Captain—Recollections of War at Sea in the Napoleonic Age 1793-1815.

LORDS OF THE SEA *by A. T. Mahan*—Great Captains of the Royal Navy During the Age of Sail.

COGGESHALL'S VOYAGES: VOLUME 1 *by George Coggeshall*—The Recollections of an American Schooner Captain.

COGGESHALL'S VOYAGES: VOLUME 2 *by George Coggeshall*—The Recollections of an American Schooner Captain.

TWILIGHT OF EMPIRE *by Sir Thomas Ussher & Sir George Cockburn*—Two accounts of Napoleon's Journeys in Exile to Elba and St. Helena: Narrative of Events by Sir Thomas Ussher & Napoleon's Last Voyage: Extract of a diary by Sir George Cockburn.

LEONAUR

ALSO FROM LEONAUR
AVAILABLE IN SOFTCOVER OR HARDCOVER WITH DUST JACKET

ESCAPE FROM THE FRENCH *by Edward Boys*—A Young Royal Navy Midshipman's Adventures During the Napoleonic War.

THE VOYAGE OF H.M.S. PANDORA *by Edward Edwards R. N. & George Hamilton, edited by Basil Thomson*—In Pursuit of the Mutineers of the Bounty in the South Seas—1790-1791.

MEDUSA *by J. B. Henry Savigny and Alexander Correard and Charlotte-Adélaïde Dard* —Narrative of a Voyage to Senegal in 1816 & The Sufferings of the Picard Family After the Shipwreck of the Medusa.

THE SEA WAR OF 1812 VOLUME 1 *by A. T. Mahan*—A History of the Maritime Conflict.

THE SEA WAR OF 1812 VOLUME 2 *by A. T. Mahan*—A History of the Maritime Conflict.

WETHERELL OF H. M. S. HUSSAR *by John Wetherell*—The Recollections of an Ordinary Seaman of the Royal Navy During the Napoleonic Wars.

THE NAVAL BRIGADE IN NATAL *by C. R. N. Burne*—With the Guns of H. M. S. Terrible & H. M. S. Tartar during the Boer War 1899-1900.

THE VOYAGE OF H. M. S. BOUNTY *by William Bligh*—The True Story of an 18th Century Voyage of Exploration and Mutiny.

SHIPWRECK! *by William Gilly*—The Royal Navy's Disasters at Sea 1793-1849.

KING'S CUTTERS AND SMUGGLERS: 1700-1855 *by E. Keble Chatterton*—A unique period of maritime history-from the beginning of the eighteenth to the middle of the nineteenth century when British seamen risked all to smuggle valuable goods from wool to tea and spirits from and to the Continent.

CONFEDERATE BLOCKADE RUNNER *by John Wilkinson*—The Personal Recollections of an Officer of the Confederate Navy.

NAVAL BATTLES OF THE NAPOLEONIC WARS *by W. H. Fitchett*—Cape St. Vincent, the Nile, Cadiz, Copenhagen, Trafalgar & Others.

PRISONERS OF THE RED DESERT *by R. S. Gwatkin-Williams*—The Adventures of the Crew of the Tara During the First World War.

U-BOAT WAR 1914-1918 *by James B. Connolly/Karl von Schenk*—Two Contrasting Accounts from Both Sides of the Conflict at Sea D uring the Great War.

www.ingramcontent.com/pod-product-compliance
Lightning Source LLC
Chambersburg PA
CBHW032054080426
42733CB00006B/271